THE Small Garden Book

THE Small Garden Book

JOHN BROOKES

Crown Publishers, Inc.
New York

Project Editor Rosie Ford

Art Editor Alex Arthur

Designer Kevin Williams

Managing Editor David Lamb

Art Director Roger Bristow

American Editor Marjorie Dietz

Published in the United States by Crown Publishers, Inc., 225 Park Avenue South, New York, New York 10003.

Published in Great Britain by Dorling Kindersley Publishers Limited.
CROWN is a trademark of Crown Publishers, Inc.

Library of Congress Cataloging-in-Publication Data

Brookes, John
    The small garden book.

    Includes index.
    1. Landscape gardening.   2. Gardens – Design.
I. Title.
SB473.B732   1989   712'.6   88-34020
ISBN 0-517-57259-1

Reproduced by Colorscan, Singapore
Printed and bound in Italy by LEGO
10 9 8 7 6 5 4 3 2 1
First Edition

CONTENTS

SMALL-GARDEN STYLE

CASE STUDIES

DESIGN

INTRODUCTION

Space is a precious commodity, so limited and expensive in towns and cities that it makes sense to enjoy every inch you have. Using outside space – be it a windowledge, roof, balcony, or basement yard – is an enjoyable, and possibly stylish way of extending the boundaries of your home.

For many the word "garden" conjures up images of lawns and herbaceous borders, soil and pruners, mulches and manures, and the niceties of horticultural technique. When presented with a tiny space, we all too often cram in all the traditional elements of a big garden, reduced in scale.

In order to make the most of a small space it is necessary to break free from preconceptions about the nature of a garden: where it should be and the things it should, or should not contain.

Gardens, first and foremost, are for people not plants. All sorts of design elements and techniques can be combined to produce a stimulating effect – planting is just one of these. Your garden might contain sculpture, some water, and a minimum of planting – lit at night the effect can be quite magical. Conversely, there can be an enormous attraction in creating a dense jungle in a tiny urban space, which not only softens the general ambiance but provides therapy in its husbandry.

The key to realizing the potential of your small space, in both visual and practical terms, is *design* – this involves planning and styling your space so that it suits your way of life, and the character of your home and its surroundings.

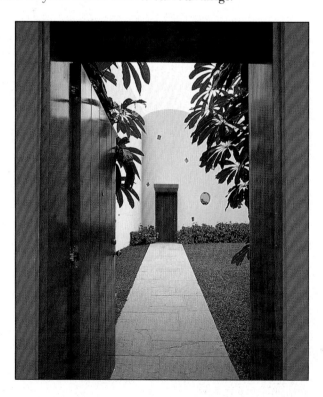

Livening up space
(above) *Nature
and architecture are
fused by the use of shape,
pattern and color.*

An illusion of size
(right) *Bold design in a
garden creates a
considerable impression
of spaciousness.*

LIVING OUTSIDE

The importance of having even a small space outside, or just a visual link with nature cannot be underestimated. A small garden, be it a balcony, roof, or terrace, is a sanctuary where you can escape the pressures of an urban existence.

Think of your space as an extension to your home, as an outside room where you can eat, read, admire a view, or watch your children play. The key to creating a sympathetic backdrop to outside living is to ask yourself first and foremost how you want to use your "room" and then, with this clear objective in mind to set about making it a pleasant place in which to be.

It is obviously easier to create a congenial outside room in Mediterranean or tropical climates, but capturing and enjoying every minute of light and warmth in more northerly climes has its own special satisfaction. However, sun alone does not make for a comfortable outside space. There are many ways it can be made inviting. Wind and draft can be minimized, ugly views concealed, privacy created and color used to make it tempting even when the sun is not shining.

Enjoying your garden from inside

Having concentrated your efforts into making use of your outside space in summer don't let them be wasted when you are inside or during the remainder of the year. Make sure your outside works visually from inside your home. Consider what it will look like from a window (not just when the sun is out), across the kitchen sink, down the hallway, or from your favorite sitting-room chair.

Small-space design

Thinking of your garden as a room also makes the concept of garden planning more approachable, for on a small scale its principles are very similar to those of interior design. Decide what you want in your space and keep the design bold and simple.

Where space is at a premium, the style and design of neither the garden nor the house can afford to work in isolation from one another. If they are complementary, restricted living space inside will benefit from the view of the garden outside and conversely a cramped garden will seem less so if it is a harmonious extension of the building it adjoins.

Roof-top (right) *A wonderful new living area has been created by enclosing this roof space and extending the tiled flooring outside.*

Sunny balcony (far right) *An abundance of planted pots has transformed this narrow wooden balcony into an inviting garden.*

Leafy-ceilinged room (left)
Dappled sunlight falls gently through the vine-entwined pergola to make this a perfect spot for leisurely meals outside.

Manipulating space (below)
Bold cubic containers line the edge of this balcony. The plants in them relate to those in the stepped beds in the garden below.

LINKING IN WITH OUT

So how do you go about establishing a harmonious link between inside and outside? Think first in terms of interlocking the spaces of the garden with the spaces of the room that adjoins it to create a flow between in and out. If you can also keep spaces in scale with one another you will be much of the way towards the desired effect. How you style the outside space can then be used to strengthen this link. For most people the design of the garden comes after deciding on interior style, so it is best to start by looking from inside out.

What style?

Ask yourself some questions. Is the room you are in period or modern? If modern, is it high-tech in style, with white walls and black chrome furniture, or is it decorated with bold colors and natural materials?

Once you have analyzed the interior, look into your garden and start to think how you can interpret that style outside. Where the mood is period, for instance, suggest the same feel in a design that accommodates period features, such as an elegant stone bench or fountain.

Strengthening the link

Now consider color. Is there a strong color scheme which would best be seen against a less demanding backdrop? Or is the room's effect neutral and able to take a strongly colored outside?

Do you have a type of flooring inside, for example, which can be used outside? If not, consider what type of exterior paving will continue the feeling of the interior flooring. Then choose artefacts that will extend the mood.

These guidelines should not become a straitjacket, however. Nobody is going to judge your garden for period authenticity. It is a place to indulge your whims and enjoy the results.

Modern mood *The sharp uncluttered lines of this modern interior are reflected in the design of the terrace. Similar paving and flooring, and the use of plant material inside and out strengthen the link.*

INTEGRATING STYLE

The views through the glass doors below show two small outside spaces that have been styled to complement the mood of the interiors they adjoin. It is important to establish a strong and stylish link between inside and outside in order to make the most effective use of your space.

Mondrian-style space
The bold patterns, simple shapes and bright primary colors of a Mondrian rug are the starting point for the design of this garden. Buttercup-yellow flooring provides the essential link between inside and out. The colors of the rug provide the inspiration for the choice of the red table and slatted blinds, the dark blue curtains and chairs, and the pale blue of the wall outside. A functioning drainpipe has been disguised between two false pipes to create an unusual sculptural feature.

Italian romance *This scene has an air of classically-inspired sophistication. The soft ochre of the walls inside and the fence outside create a gentle backdrop to the strong pattern of the black-and-white checkered flooring. A dramatic swagged curtain gives an aura of grandeur to the scene, echoed by the round stone table and the classical bust on the wall. The simple white chairs are as suitable for use inside as outside. Their moss-green upholstery links the eye with the elegant cypress that conceals the drainpipe.*

GARDEN, WHAT GARDEN?

It is all very well, you might think, for those with neat little walled yards, but what about those with a drafty side access, a dark light well or only a windowledge – spaces that could never be called a garden, nor thought of as an outside room? Garden them in the traditional sense you cannot, but improve them you certainly may.

Because many such areas are initially unattractive they are neglected and allowed to become dark, dank, or damp, particularly if they are below ground level. It may be that a flight of dingy basement steps is your only outside space. Rather than letting them detract from your surroundings turn them into an asset – a pleasure to walk through and look at from inside or from the street.

There are many different ways of enlivening unattractive places. Planting is one of them, but it shouldn't be the first option to spring to mind. Consider a lick of paint – use a vibrant color, paint a pattern, or even a *trompe l'oeil* (see p.73). Improve the flooring and the lighting too.

Leftover spaces that appear small on a plan are often contained by overpoweringly high walls. Consider a way of "bringing the ceiling down".

Pergola beams may darken the space, but stretched ropes or wires are lighter and you can run a foliaged climber over them, thereby creating a congenial space, albeit small, into which to escape outside for an evening drink.

Doorstep and window gardens

The decorative potential of doors and windows that link us with the outside world often remains unrealized. A few pots on a windowledge and a colored windowframe can act as a visual extension to your room by breaking down the barriers between in and out. If you live on a top floor use your window to frame a treetop view – if you don't have a garden, borrow one.

The technique for dealing with odd spaces successfully is not one of cut-price gardening, rather it is one of theater, where props, illusion, light and color can be used to create a lively place.

Appealing passageway (right) *A narrow passageway has been widened visually by strong lateral lines of brick paving. The plants in pots can be moved into full light from time to time.*

Doorstep garden *Good use has been made of a limited space by training variegated ivies* (Hedera canariensis *'Gloire de Marengo'*), *planted in two simple pots, around a front entrance.*

Stairway space *A recessed planting box containing a basic evergreen planting of* Aucuba japonica *and ivy, enlivens a city stairway, and is ideal for "prettying up" with annuals for temporary color accents.*

A TRANSFORMATION

The photographs on this page and on the following six show the transformation of a small and run-down garden into an inviting and congenial outside room. Design is the key to the successful transformation of small-space gardens. This involves planning a layout structured to suit your needs and to complement the character of your home and its surroundings.

Design criteria

There is no blue-print design that will work in every small garden, for there are so many variable factors: your life style and the way in which you wish to use the space, your likes and dislikes *vis à vis* styles of structure and planting, the limitations of the site, the character of the surroundings, and the amount of money you have to spend on materials and plants.

When planning your space you will need to take all these factors, and more, into consideration and then go on to find a way to encompass them all in a single design that fits the bill. Planning is an important stage in the process of transforming a garden – it is worth investing plenty of time at this stage so that you find a design that satisfies you in the long-run.

The garden shown here lies at the rear of a nineteenth-century terrace house in a busy town just outside central London. The owners have two small children and they wanted to get

The existing garden
(above) *The garden was divided into two equally uninviting areas, both dominated by the walls.*

The garden transformed
(right) *The new design makes every part of the garden a pleasure to use and gives it a roomy feel.*

maximum use from the space: to enjoy meals in the open air, to use the area for small gatherings as well as for holding larger parties, and, most importantly, to create an environment in which the children could safely play in view of the house.

The existing garden

The existing arrangement of the garden was unsatisfactory on all fronts. There was a harsh division between two areas, neither of which was conducive to use: a sunken paved area which was damp and shady (and though linked to the large kitchen by a glazed door, was not a pleasant area in which to eat) and an area of scruffy grass dominated by the boundary walls.

Making visual use of space

Visibility from the kitchen dining-area was restricted by the retaining walls to a somewhat dismal view of the sunken paved area, meaning the rest of the garden was wasted in visual terms, and the view from the reception room on the ground floor and the bedrooms on the floors above was uninspiring to say the least. To combat this the whole area was, broadly speaking, opened out. The original grass area was lowered by excavating considerable quantities of soil. It was then linked to

The results of design (top, right, far right and below) *The dramatic effect that design had on this poorly-planned garden, top, is apparent in these photographs. The retaining walls of the original paved area were lowered and access to (and a view of) the rest of the garden was allowed by building a low flight of steps, right. The inside/outside effect is furthered by the use of paving, far right, to create four "rooms" at different levels and by the use of garden furniture. The designer's impression, below, shows the aim of the planting is to soften the angular structures.*

The plan (below) *The geometrical pattern of the new structures can be seen here in relation to the areas of planting.*

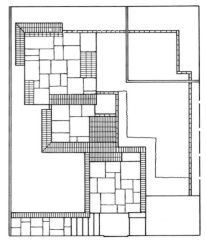

View one – before *When looking across the garden from this angle the eye is inevitably drawn down into the dank paved area that dominates the view.*

View one – the new structure *The design begins to take shape with the opening up of the paved area, allowing the eye to take in the whole garden.*

View two – before *From this angle the eye is led by the wall and fence boundaries, across the ill-defined grassy area to a corner of no interest.*

View two – the new structure *The gently rising steps allow the garden to be seen as a whole, rather than as two rigidly-defined areas.*

View three – before *Seen from the rear, the garden is not much more than a patch of lackluster lawn. At night the yard was almost invisible.*

View three – the new structure *Once the yard has been replaced by these wide, shallow steps, the apparent length of the garden is exaggerated.*

View one – after six months
(left) *In time, the foreground plant material (recently planted) will fill out so it is in scale with the hard materials.*

View one – designer's impression

View two – after six months
(left) *The garden looks much softer after planting; the lawn sits neatly into the pattern created by the paving and planting.*

View two – designer's impression

View three – after six months
(left) *The paved area provides a pleasant eating/sitting area, furthering the overall "outside room" effect.*

View three – designer's impression

the sunken paved area by a series of gentle changes in level. This meant that better use could be made of the space available and the whole of the garden became visible from the basement. It also made the new grassed area a lot safer for the children to play on, for the large drop between this level and the original sunken area was greatly reduced. The hard structures of the garden created a framework for the areas of planting; shown here after six months it is already softening the whole effect and as it matures it will reinforce the structural pattern.

The transformation

The stepped levels create a sculptural effect and the angular arrangement of the retaining walls (which can also be used as seating) are echoed in the shape of the built-in brick bench which defines

The finished product *A view of the new garden from the rear wall – it is difficult to imagine this as the unattractive, uninviting space it once was.*

the eating area and saves the clutter of too many free-standing chairs. An area of grass was retained for the children to play on; its geometrical shape is an integral part of the garden's pattern. To maximize the pleasure you get from your small garden you should think about what it looks like from inside, both at ground level and from above.

To make a strong visual link between the garden and the house, the honey-colored house wall brick was used to build the new walls, the steps and the bench seat. Soft-colored stone slabs were chosen for the paving, to tone in with the mellow brick of the house.

SMALL-GARDEN STYLE

The smallest of garden spaces should have style — a style that suits you and the way you live, as well as the character of your home and its surroundings.

Advice for choosing a style and how to use it to the best effect in your outside space is followed by a review of five small gardens, each of which will inspire you with its distinct style.

ROOM FOR STYLE

Style is an evocative word which conjures up a galaxy of images, ranging from people and places to cars and clothes.

I identify style in a garden space where there is a clarity of purpose that is derived from an aesthetically pleasing arrangement of shapes and patterns. Some styles might not be to your particular taste but, by virtue of the fact they make a positive and coherent statement visually, you might happily acknowledge that they "have style".

But how do you relate such abstracts to your small garden when there are so many practical factors to take into account, such as the location and boundaries of the site, the style of your home, and most importantly, how you want to use the space?

The art lies in treating each element of your garden – be it the walls, furniture, steps, or a plant pot – as part of a single design. Always bear in mind how one relates to another in terms of color, shape and texture, as well as function. A piecemeal approach – building a raised bed here, planting a shrub there – and an assortment of ill-considered bits and pieces will result in what I would consider an unstylish mishmash, and also make a space seem smaller. A successful small garden, whether it be at ground level or on a balcony or roof-top, is one in which all its elements, from the smallest to the biggest, are in accord.

Do not let the size of your garden make you timid in your design. Be bold and give it style.

Gothic garden (above)
This individual creation may not be to your taste but certainly has style.

Stylish contrast (right)
A refreshing combination of town architecture and relaxed, textured planting.

WHAT MAKES A STYLE?

Understanding the essence of a look is the secret to breathing style into your small garden. As the photographs on these pages show, the cottage garden style (to take one very popular garden style as an example) can be interpreted in different ways. There is no set of rules or clever formulae which govern how this is done. Instead the art lies in having sensitivity to an overall picture and how detail fits into this.

Understanding a style's hallmarks

The classic cottage garden has a homely, rural image of roses rambling round a door, and relaxed country planting. Many gardeners try to emulate this style, but all too often they miss their mark and find themselves with just a messy hodge-podge of planting. This is because the apparently relaxed disorder of country planting is in fact quite controlled, for it is contained within a strong underlying framework.

In the true cottage garden the color of walls, paintwork and roofing, and the texture of brick, clay, or stone are all strongly evident. These strong structural elements are overlaid by soft, gentle, masses of plant material. The cottage garden look, whether it be in Devon or Long Island, is created by the combination of the shapes, textures and colors of hard materials with the soft ones of plants. Local building materials, artefacts and native plants will give each a distinct character but the hallmarks of the style are the same.

Interpreting style

Feel free to extract the essence of a style and interpret it in your small garden. A well-known look can quite easily be given an amusing twist, such as using vegetables decoratively or including a lighthearted piece of sculpture.

If your space is very limited, just a few of the characteristics of a style can be effectively combined. You might, for instance, group a few brightly-colored cylindrical containers planted with yuccas for a high-tech feel, or use a mossy stone statue for a classical look.

The inspiration (left) *An unselfconscious grouping of pots and plants in a quiet country corner.*

Town version (above) *Racemes of* Laburnum *sp. and a tumble of roses bring a breath of country air to this garden.*

Thoughtful interpretation (right) *Delicate clouds of London pride and snow-in-summer contrast with gray sheets of slate.*

NATIONAL GARDEN STYLES

There are distinct national styles of gardens – Italian, French, Spanish, Indian, Japanese, English, and central European, as well as those of America, which have evolved from regions of the East and West Coasts, the South and Southwest and Middle West. Looking at how different styles have evolved is one way of introducing yourself to the many exciting ways of styling your outside space.

Reflecting building and life styles

The character of gardens around the world are closely linked to the local styles of buildings. The scale and shape of surrounding structures often give the garden character – low flat buildings an open look, tall narrow ones an enclosed feel. Architectural idioms are often echoed in the detailing of a garden as well as the design of its layout. The color and texture of the materials used are an intrinsic part of the look too.

As well as echoing building styles, gardens reflect different ways of life and traditions. The design of the Japanese garden, for instance, has religious symbolism, and that of the North African garden, as well as providing a cool retreat from the heat, has a geometry and pattern which is traditionally Islamic.

The influence of natural phenomena

It is often native vegetation that gives us the strongest impression of place. Conifers and birch immediately make us think of cold climes, and palms and large cacti of hot, dry locations. Vegetation is closely followed by the quality of light in a region. Strong light from a sun high in the sky creates hard-edged, deep shadows, whereas with a softer light we are more conscious of its warming glow. Closer to the Poles, crisp sunlight from lower in the sky casts long shadows.

"Ethnic" styles

I loosely term gardens that derive their style solely from the character of local features, such as the buildings, plants, and artefacts rather than a consciously-designed layout, "ethnic". The desert look is one of these styles. The African version, which takes its flavor from the beaten red earth, native pots, and tough plants, has counterparts in Rajusthan and Mexico. There is a tropical look too, common to parts of Africa and the West Indies.

Western styles

In the West, our images of different garden styles are linked to historical period as well as place. In the seventeenth century, European gardens had a formal layout, which was an extension of the logic of classical architecture. Formal Italian gardens thus have a distinct seventeenth-century feel.

In the eighteenth century an awareness of the Chinese garden and its abstracted, though natural, formation began to disconcert the European eye. When mixed with the increasing loosening-up of baroque architecture, and the asymmetry of rococo, the result was a more organic and flowing style of garden. The nineteenth century saw a mixture of formality and looser shapes, in gardens of a smaller scale.

Among the myriad of contemporary styles there is the Californian outdoor-living look associated with the late 1950s, and the wildflower or prairie look which is identified with the 1980s.

Although there is greater strength in a homogenous approach, the elements of distinct garden styles can be combined to a degree. A contrast of styles can work well too. Such steps are sometimes successful when it comes to developing your own style, as you will see on the following pages.

Mexican style *The strong architectural forms of this dominating entrance are well complemented by strong natural ones. The cacti and succulents cast dramatic shadows on the adobe walls, and the group of terracotta pots accentuates the broad sweep of the traditionally-patterned brickwork.*

Japanese garden (above) *The standard back garden of this town house has been transformed into a serene and contemplative sanctuary. The asymmetric pattern of the stones, ragged brick paving and loosely-laid gravel combine to give the garden a gentle, abstract rhythm.*

Mediterranean mood (left) *A domestic scene can be glimpsed at the end of this cool, sunlit passageway. Washing dries beneath a vine, and plants grow in an assortment of old pots and tins, painted blue, like the wall.*

ITALIAN-STYLE GARDEN

This small formal garden has a classic Italianate style. The central, water-filled courtyard is surrounded by a covered walkway, one end of which leads to a reception hall.

The courtyard pattern is composed of four brick "island" beds, and square stepping stones symmetrically arranged around an urn-shaped fountain raised on a stone plinth.

The "island" beds, filled with colorful annuals (yellow lily-flowered tulips (*Tulipa* cvs.) in the spring followed by white snapdragon (*Antirrhinum* cvs.) in the summer) and surrounded by neatly-trimmed box hedge, are linked to the tiled walkway by stepping stones that provide access for maintenance. Water lilies grow from submerged planting boxes, and flowering evergreens flourish beneath the walkway.

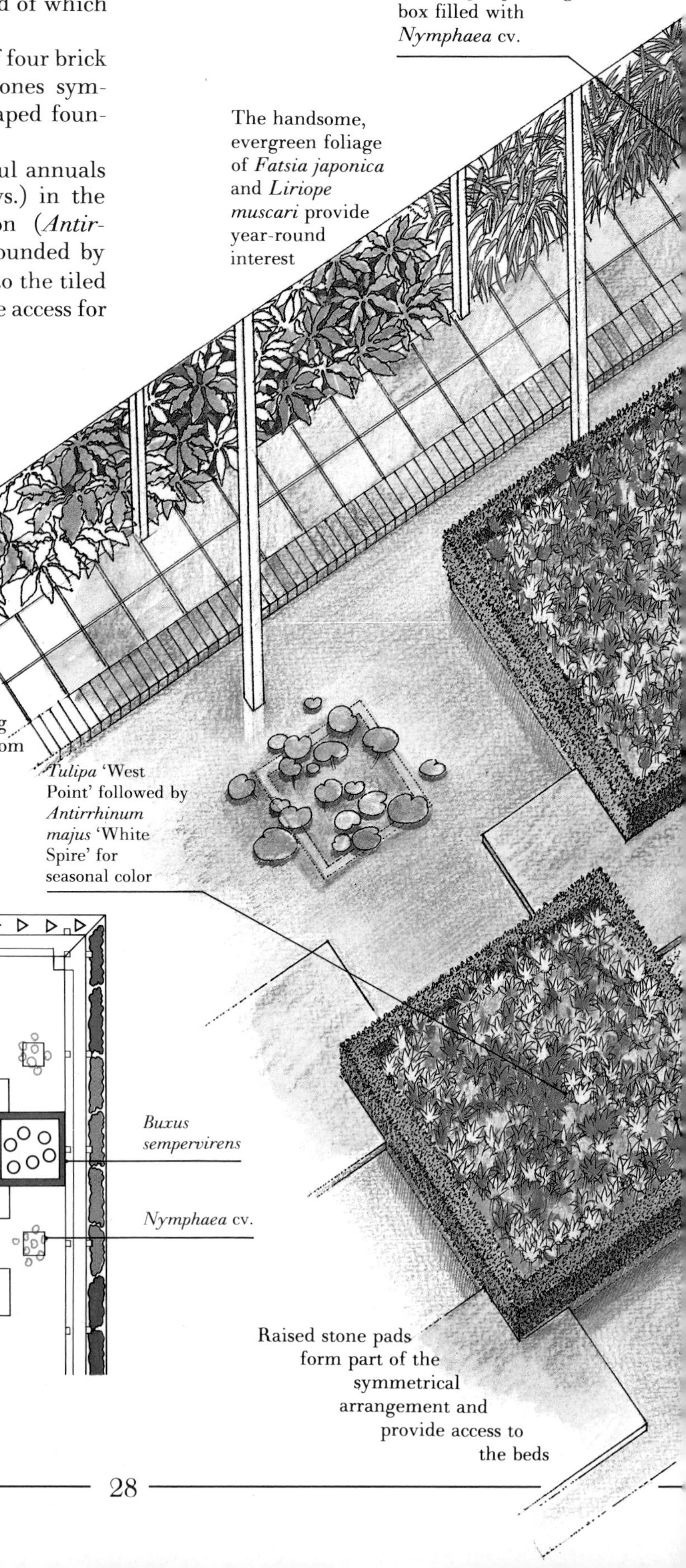

Submerged planting box filled with *Nymphaea* cv.

The handsome, evergreen foliage of *Fatsia japonica* and *Liriope muscari* provide year-round interest

Terracotta tiles like those used in adjoining reception room

Tulipa 'West Point' followed by *Antirrhinum majus* 'White Spire' for seasonal color

Hedera colchica 'Dentata Variegata'

Fatsia japonica

Liriope muscari

Tulipa 'West Point' followed by *Antirrhinum majus* 'White Spire'

Buxus sempervirens

Nymphaea cv.

Raised stone pads form part of the symmetrical arrangement and provide access to the beds

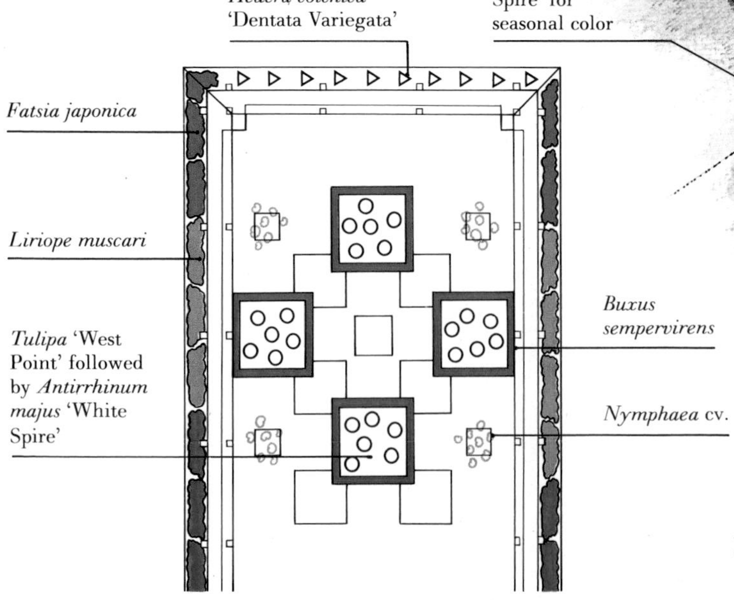

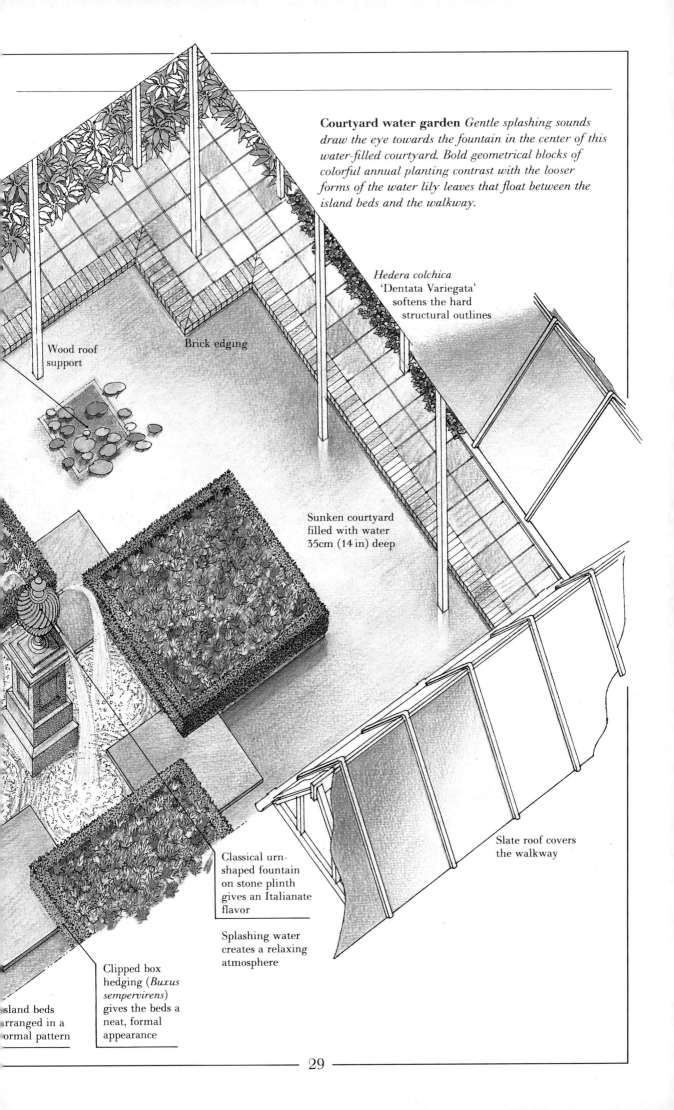

Courtyard water garden *Gentle splashing sounds draw the eye towards the fountain in the center of this water-filled courtyard. Bold geometrical blocks of colorful annual planting contrast with the looser forms of the water lily leaves that float between the island beds and the walkway.*

Hedera colchica 'Dentata Variegata' softens the hard structural outlines

Wood roof support

Brick edging

Sunken courtyard filled with water 35cm (14 in) deep

Slate roof covers the walkway

Classical urn-shaped fountain on stone plinth gives an Italianate flavor

Splashing water creates a relaxing atmosphere

Clipped box hedging (*Buxus sempervirens*) gives the beds a neat, formal appearance

sland beds rranged in a ormal pattern

WHAT IS YOUR STYLE?

It is not always easy when faced with such a wide variety of garden styles to decide which one would best suit your small plot. It is hard too, when looking at a site, to envisage how it can be transformed into anything stylish. Looking at your personal style, and that of the building you live in will point you in the right direction.

Interpreting your style outside

Seek to evolve a style outside that suits your personality, for your garden, like your clothes or your sitting room, should be an expression of your own taste. It may be that you go for the clear-cut look, or perhaps a relaxed muddly effect. An urban French couple, for example, might well find the randomness of an English garden hard to cope with, hating the apparent disorder, whilst, conversely, someone happy in this type of garden might find the clipped, classic order of a typical French garden too disciplined and restrictive.

The design of your garden should be suited to your life style too. Ask yourself how much time or inclination you have to tend plants. If you are green-fingered and enjoy nurturing plants, then provide yourself with plenty of greenery, room for your gardening equipment and a table for potting-up. If, on the other hand, you have a hectic schedule that leaves little time for gardening or spend a lot of time away from your home, you would be better suited to a garden that requires little maintenance. Such a garden relies on the textures and colors of its structure, and perhaps a *trompe l'oeil* or a piece of sculpture, and a few large plants in pots to provide the interest.

Using your space

Decide also how you want to *use* your outside space. Do you for instance enjoy entertaining outside and want a table, chairs and a barbecue, or do you need space for your children to play, or even a small dog to run in?

There are many ways of styling outside space so you can get maximum use from it. You might, for instance, have a space that gets little sun and is not very conducive to day-time use, but that planted with lilies and other scented plants makes a

Shaded bower *A stone path leads through a mass of Jerusalem sage* (Phlomis fruticosa) *to a white Lutyens bench in the midst of a romantically-planted bower.*

Summery colors *The soft, sunny blues and pinks of this Floridian entrance terrace create just the right mood for summertime relaxation.*

fragrant evening retreat. Or perhaps you have an urban roof-space that gets full sun, but howling winds too. Style a space like this to give you some shelter and also an air of privacy.

Looking at buildings

We live in a bewildering variety of structures, ranging from all kinds of town houses, detached or terraced, to apartment blocks, including every size of unit, and the infinite variety of suburban housing. The spectrum of architectural styles spans from those of the eighteenth and nineteenth centuries to 20's Modern, 40's Utility, 70's high-tech, and 80's neoclassic.

The style of your home will probably have already influenced your choice of interior decorations and furnishings. Let it do the same for your garden. Every architectural style has idioms which can be expressed in the line and form of the garden's layout, whatever its size, and the selection of materials from which it is made, be it stone, cement or brick.

The choice and grouping of pots and furnishings can be an extension of that style, as can the plants that soften the overall effect. You can be purist in your selection and historically accurate in each and every detail, or simply engender the general mood of a style.

Sculptured space *The bold and functional style of this German garden complements the architecture of the house. Big blocks of irregularly-shaped concrete lead the way through a mass of cobbles to a striking crimson piece of sculpture raised on a massive stone block – not a garden for the timid.*

GARDENS TO LIVE IN

The notion that the garden, no matter how small or awkward the location, should be a place where plants reign supreme, or even a scaled-down version of a nineteenth-century country garden is becoming increasingly impractical and outdated.

The best use can be made of a small garden space if its structures – walls, steps, pools, and furniture – become attractive features of the garden in their own right, and plants, rather than dominating the garden or being its *raison d'être*, are used as decoration.

By the time you have created a pleasant spot for dining and another in which to sunbathe, the amount of space left for plants will have been considerably diminished. Introduce a fashionable hot tub, jacuzzi, or plunge pool and the conventional image of the garden as a leafy retreat starts to take on quite a new form.

Increasing apparent size

As well as using space economically, there are many ways of increasing the apparent size of your small plot. A good first step is to extend the feel of the garden inside your home. For instance, placing tubs of plants on a small paved area, and on the floor of an adjoining room, will blur the division between inside and out. Using the same, or similar tones of color on inside walls as you use on outside walls will have the same effect.

It is an all too common misconception that small spaces are suited to an abundance of small objects. In fact, this usually creates a cluttered look and can make a very tiny enclosed space seem distinctly claustrophobic. As the art of the interior decorator shows, the fewer the number of objects in a small room and the simpler the range of colors and fabrics, the larger it will appear.

The same principle should be applied outside to create the same effect. Limit the number of objects and structures in your garden, and scale them up, rather than down. Stick to a simple range of materials, preferably matching them to existing structures, such as boundary fencing or the walls of your home. Build in as many features as possible and decorate the garden with a carefully chosen selection of plants, grouped in bold masses.

Rural terrace (above) *Growing plants above and around this tiny terrace, rather than on it, leaves room for dining and relaxing* al fresco.

Italian courtyard (right) *The "arches" on the courtyard wall link outside with inside and, together with a small range of plants, provide stylish decoration.*

TWO-TIER TOWN GARDEN

This small two-tier garden lies at the back of an Edwardian town house. Originally, a rusty metal stairway led from a narrow balcony to a shabby grassed area below. Because there was no visual link between the two they were viewed quite separately. The aim of the design was to unify the two, making the whole area appear more spacious and to create a stylish pocket of calm within a busy urban environment.

Styling the new structures

The metal balcony and stairway were replaced by a new structure. Wood was used in order to forge a strong visual link with the wooden door and window surrounds. The patterning of the cross bars is in the idiom of the architectural style of the house. Sage-green paintwork echoes the Art Nouveau flavor of the interior decor. The balcony was widened to accommodate chairs from the reception room from which it leads. The higher end section of the balcony railing, covered with a climber, screens the balcony from passers-by in the alleyway that runs alongside the house.

At ground level stone was chosen to replace the area of grass. Using a hard surfacing unifies the area with the structure of the house; its mellow color blends in with the soft green paintwork.

A climber growing up the balcony links the two tiers, and along with other plants and an existing tree give the garden an air of freshness. The overall effect is of a calm and simple retreat amongst urban surroundings.

Two-tier garden *A new wooden balcony and steps (designed to complement the architecture of the house) replace an unstylish metal structure, and old stone paving the once shabby grassed area below. Small unpaved areas are left for plants. The balcony acts as an outdoor extension to the reception room and the paved terrace to the basement games room.*

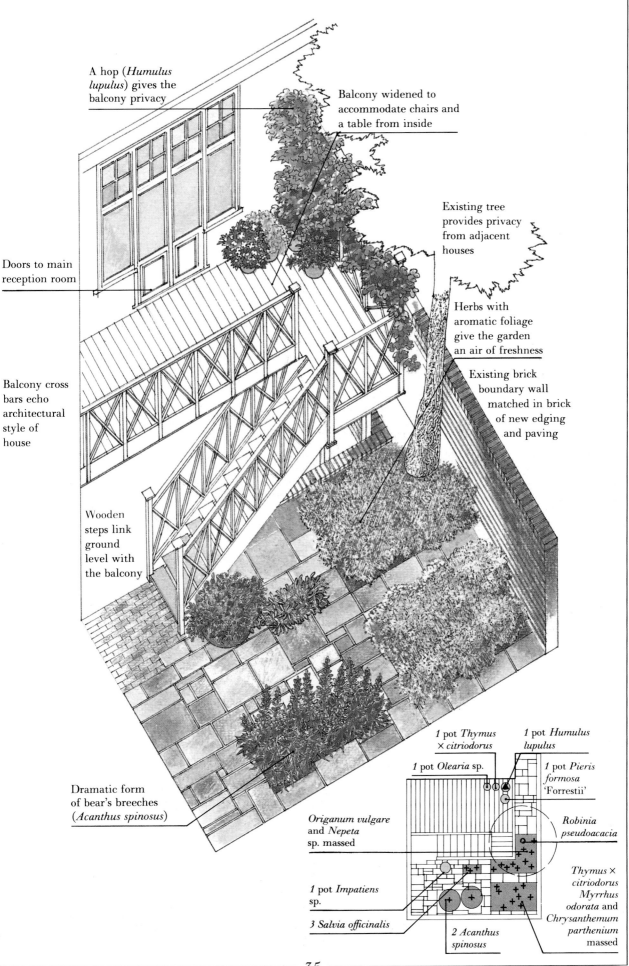

A hop (*Humulus lupulus*) gives the balcony privacy

Balcony widened to accommodate chairs and a table from inside

Existing tree provides privacy from adjacent houses

Doors to main reception room

Herbs with aromatic foliage give the garden an air of freshness

Balcony cross bars echo architectural style of house

Existing brick boundary wall matched in brick of new edging and paving

Wooden steps link ground level with the balcony

Dramatic form of bear's breeches (*Acanthus spinosus*)

1 pot *Thymus × citriodorus*

1 pot *Humulus lupulus*

1 pot *Olearia* sp.

1 pot *Pieris formosa* 'Forrestii'

Origanum vulgare and *Nepeta* sp. massed

Robinia pseudoacacia

1 pot *Impatiens* sp.

Thymus × citriodorus Myrrhus odorata and *Chrysanthemum parthenium* massed

3 *Salvia officinalis*

2 *Acanthus spinosus*

GARDENS JUST TO LOOK AT

The juxtaposition of buildings in towns and cities leave many people with small, awkwardly-shaped and often unappealingly-located spaces, which, though visible from inside their homes, they cannot, or have no inclination to use as an outside room. Any such dingy yard, narrow passageway or deep well can be transformed from an area from which the eyes are hastily averted to one that is a positive pleasure to look at.

Decorating small spaces

There are many ways of bringing to life such spaces. Restricted light and difficult access often make gardening in the traditional way impractical, so instead of decorating your space just with plants, consider using colored paint, mirrors, sculpture, *trompe l'oeil* effects, and artificial light.

It is important that the ground plan of your space should bear a relationship to surrounding structures, so start by looking at the paving. See if there are any architectural features on surrounding buildings that can be linked to the style of the paving – polychrome brickwork, for example, might suggest multicolored floor tiling.

Your next task should be to make the best use of the space by making it eye-catching. Using sculpture is one of the most simple and effective ways of anchoring the eye in a space (see pp.134–5). Make sure that whatever you choose (be it a classical stone statue or a modern abstract piece) has visual strength and is not dominated by its surroundings. Introduce the type of feature you might envisage in a more open space, but go for as large a scale as you can to make the effect.

Plants are seldom visually strong enough to assume a sculptural role, nor in many cases are they a practical proposition where light is poor and their location makes regular maintenance a problem. However, given reasonable growing conditions, a gnarled fig tree might work for instance, as long as the structure of its natural form is visually linked to the ground-pattern and surrounding structures so that it does not appear awkwardly isolated.

Window view (above) *This tiny fenced space has been transformed by rocks, pebbles, ferns and the sculptural shape of an* Acer japonicum *into a textural composition to be enjoyed from within the bathtub.*

Tiny yard (right) *A trompe l'oeil of paint and trelliswork has been used to transform the shape of a tiny, bleak yard. Hanging ferns (a Boston and a maidenhair), a mossy cherub and a miniscule pool of still water complete the composition.*

Even something as simple as a large boulder can assume a sculptural quality. Put it next to a hollow fiberglass boulder that is illuminated at night and you really have something unusual. You may recoil in horror at this idea, but if the nature of the space is artificial, why not the artifacts in it?

Tricking the eye

Trompe l'oeil is an effective way of disguising reality and introducing a theatrical feel to a limited space. The Renaissance Italians were past masters at providing amusing diversions not only in their gardens, in the form of statues, but also visual tricks painted on their walls – a tiny monkey peering through a balustrade, or someone waving from an upper window. Similar techniques can be used to add an element of fun and magic to a space visible from your home.

Paint can be used in a simpler way too. Colored walls can bring light and vitality to the most unappealing of spaces. Painting a space

outside the same color as the room from which it is seen will make a strong link between the two.

The reflections from strategically placed mirrors can trick the eye too, making a space appear larger, or lighter, or as in the illustration below, to obscure an unwanted view. Artificial lighting is an effective way of enlivening a space that is dull during the day and giving it a magical touch at night (see pp.136–7).

Alternatives to planting

If growing conditions are too poor for real plants why not paint some on your wall instead, or if the amount of space limits the number of plants you can grow paint some of a similar type on a wall.

Alternatively, you can decorate your space with cut flowers arranged in a simply-shaped container. Dried flowers can be striking too; perhaps a mass of huge allium heads, teasels, or even pampas grass is just what is needed to give your dark corner an atmospheric Edwardian look.

Small, city space *Three sides of a city home face a small yard that backs on to a rather run-down house used as an office/warehouse. Two window-frames and a door-frame like those of the building have been used*

to create a surreal effect. The mirrored window-frame reflects the feature and view inside, whilst hiding the ugly drainpipe. The unmirrored door-frame on the left echoes the French windows.

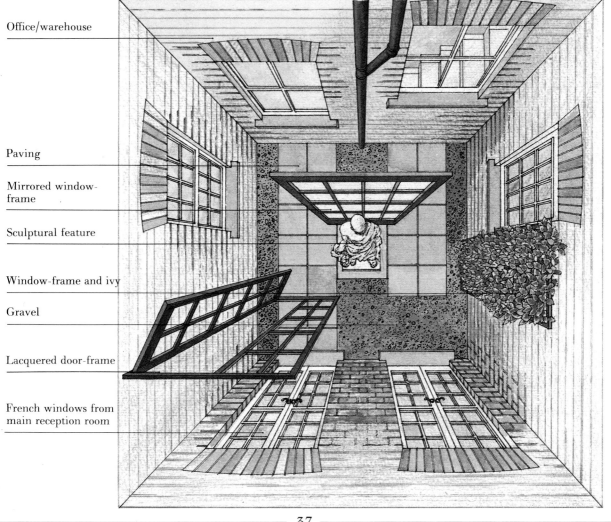

Office/warehouse

Paving

Mirrored window-frame

Sculptural feature

Window-frame and ivy

Gravel

Lacquered door-frame

French windows from main reception room

NEW LIVING SPACE

The area now occupied by this garden was once used as a parking space and the house it adjoins was a stable block. The new interior was designed first. A kitchen and living room, built in the downstairs area, were given opening glass doors to allow easy access to the garden and to maximize the view of it from inside. The garden was designed to create an area that worked as an open-air extension of the kitchen and living room, where meals could be enjoyed and to which the owner felt closely connected when inside the house.

Designing the structure

To make the area work as an extension it was necessary to forge a strong link between inside and outside. This was done by echoing the dimensions of the kitchen in the terrace area. The kitchen ceiling is continued outside in the form of a pergola, the same height. The door, window surrounds and pergola are all of the same unplaned, stained timber. Dark wooden tubs on the paved area extend the visual link to ground level.

The pergola gives the area beneath it a pleasant room-like quality, reinforced by the climbers which clothe the wall to its side. Two lights create a warm glow that gently illuminates the area, creating an atmosphere conducive to sitting outside on

Corner detail (above)
Two planted containers in front of a Scotch thistle create an area of dramatic interest.

Extended living (right)
A wooden pergola, draped with ivy, defines the paved area which is used as an extension to the kitchen.

summer evenings, and enabling the area to be seen from inside the house at night, thereby maximizing enjoyment of the garden. The lights will be especially appreciated during the winter months, when darkness falls early.

The choice of materials

The area is surfaced with paving and gravel. The width of the area paved with concrete slabs is the same as the width of the kitchen, and the width of each slab relates to the width of the door panels; this reinforces the inside-outside link. The honey color of the new slabs tones in well with the smaller, original stable tiles that were retained adjacent to the kitchen. These tiles were laid in a rhythmic pattern across an existing tiled drainage gulley and into the area of new paving beyond the sliding doors of the house.

Areas of pale brown gravel tone in well with the paving and contrast with planting in two brick-edged beds and in the gravel. The area along the boundary wall was excavated, filled with earth and edged with brick that matches the exterior wall of the kitchen.

The use of plants

Gold- and silver-foliaged plants contrast with both the dark wood of the pergola, and the window and door detailing. In conjunction with the pale gravel and paving, the plants give the area a bright, sunlit feel. Two trees were planted, both of which have light-colored foliage: a silver-leaved *Eucalyptus gunnii* between the two pergola horizontals nearest the house, and a golden *Catalpa bignonioides* 'Aurea' on the right (looking towards the house). The theme of gold is continued in many of the plants, including *Alchemilla mollis*, which bears green-yellow flowers, and golden-yellow *Euphorbia wulfenii*. The theme of silver is continued in *Helichrysum petiolatum* 'Limelight', *Stachys lanata*, and *Artemisia* 'Powis Castle'. *Hosta* sp. and cvs. and other plants with architectural form such as *Yucca recurvifolia* form a strong, structural backbone that supports softer-style plants, such as catmint (*Nepeta* × *faassenii*) and *Alchemilla mollis*.

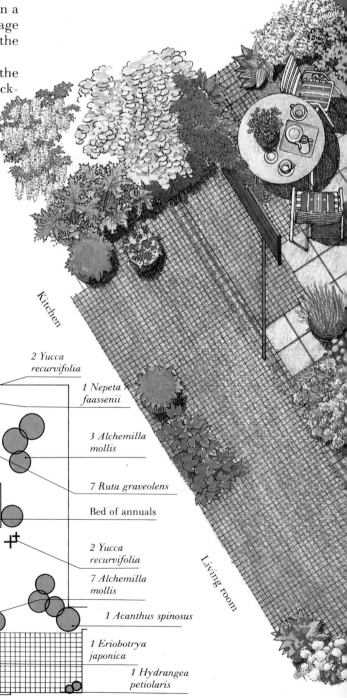

1 *Catalpa bignoniodes*

3 *Stachys lanata*

2 *Euphorbia wulfenii*

2 *Yucca recurvifolia*

1 *Rosa* 'Nevada'

1 *Choisya ternata*

1 *Trachycarpus fortunei*

1 *Hedera canariensis* 'Gloire de Marengo'

1 *Choisya ternata* 'Sundance'

1 *Artemisia* 'Powis Castle'

1 *Hosta fortunei*

2 *Libertia formosa*

1 *Eucalyptus gunnii*

2 *Rheum palmatum*

Kitchen

1 *Nepeta × faassenii*

3 *Alchemilla mollis*

7 *Ruta graveolens*

Bed of annuals

2 *Yucca recurvifolia*

7 *Alchemilla mollis*

1 *Acanthus spinosus*

1 *Eriobotrya japonica*

1 *Hydrangea petiolaris*

Living room

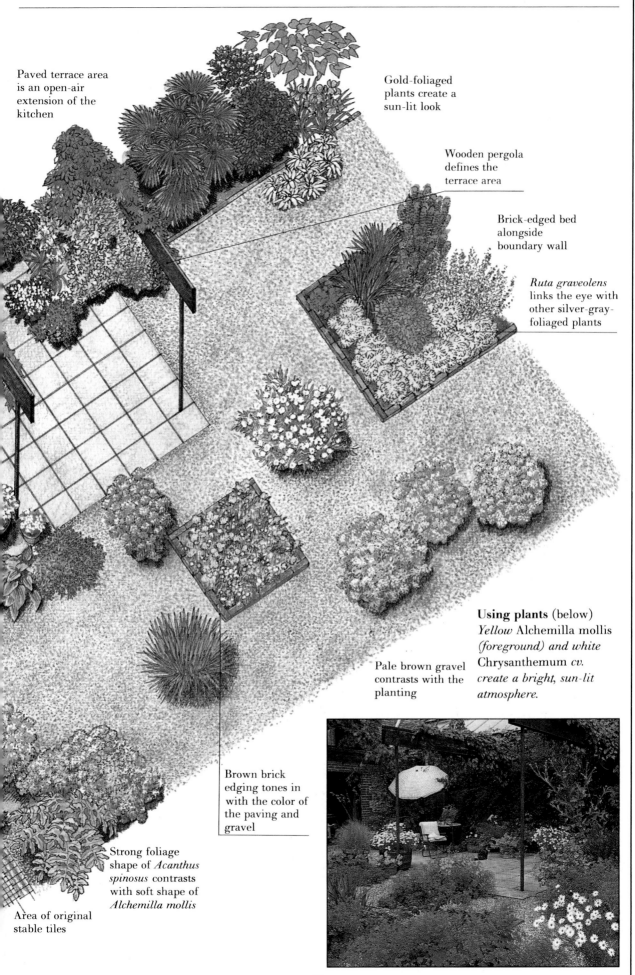

Paved terrace area is an open-air extension of the kitchen

Gold-foliaged plants create a sun-lit look

Wooden pergola defines the terrace area

Brick-edged bed alongside boundary wall

Ruta graveolens links the eye with other silver-gray-foliaged plants

Using plants (below) *Yellow* Alchemilla mollis *(foreground) and white* Chrysanthemum *cv.* *create a bright, sun-lit atmosphere.*

Pale brown gravel contrasts with the planting

Brown brick edging tones in with the color of the paving and gravel

Strong foliage shape of *Acanthus spinosus* contrasts with soft shape of *Alchemilla mollis*

Area of original stable tiles

CLASSIC CHIC

The strong structure of this small town garden prevents it from being overwhelmed by the huge London plane tree (*Platanus* × *acerifolia*) which towers over it, and anchors the eye within the site. This garden is one of a row backing on to a terrace of five- or six-story houses. The tree relates in scale to these, and though it casts much of the garden in shade, it does also give it some privacy from overlooking neighboring houses.

Design logic

The Italian designers who own this nineteenth-century house have decorated and furnished the interior in a very sophisticated modern style. This is reflected in the clean, well-defined lines of the garden's layout. Most of the surfaces are constructed from brick, like that of the house, thereby sympathetically linking the two. When the tree has shed its leaves the garden can be seen clearly from the main reception room and the various bedrooms and family rooms above, so I devised a layout with a geometrical pattern which looks pleasing from every level.

The owners wanted their garden to be congenial for summer entertaining and for family lunches in the area at the far end, which briefly gets the sun. I included two paved areas for seating, therefore, on the left-hand side of the garden.

Bird's eye view (above)
Paving and gravel make a visually exciting pattern from above.

Using pattern (right)
An L-shaped area of planted gravel links the two seating areas.

The right-hand side of the garden is clear of furniture so that an awning can be rigged up from the entrance and along the side wall, for parties on special occasions. The entrance to the garden is down steps at the end of a hall which runs the full length of the house. The uncluttered view from here to the end of the garden accentuates this strong visual axis.

Structure and planting

The site was originally grassed over except for areas of perimeter planting. To have floored the whole area in brick would have given the garden a very hard look, so areas of washed pea gravel (toned brown) were introduced to soften the overall effect. The brick flooring, set in concrete, forms a series of pads which link the house to the paved sitting areas at either end of the garden.

The existing areas of perimeter planting were not abandoned but the original brick retaining walls were rebuilt to a height of 75cm (30 in), making ideal casual seating.

In order to make the basement dining room lighter, an area 3m (10 ft) long was dug out immediately in front of it. A brick plinth, three-quarters of the way down the garden can be seen from this room. At present home to a tub of annuals, it will eventually be the base for a sculptural feature. The plinth also forms one edge

of a built-in seat. Though the owners design smart Italian furniture, they decided to opt for something more traditional in the form of a teak bench surface, which rests on the built-in brick seat, and a free-standing teak table and chairs.

There are plenty of shade-tolerant plants, such as ferns, bamboos, and ivies, because much of this garden is in deep shade while the rest only gets intermittent light.

Most of the planting is confined to the raised beds, leaving plenty of space in the middle of the garden for summer entertaining. Gravel planting, as illustrated on page 206, (including *Alchemilla mollis* and *Iris foetidissima*) prevents this area from looking too stark, while a great variety of evergreen planting (including *Choisya ternata* and *Skimmia japonica*) provides year-round interest. The bold groupings of plant material relate in scale to the layout and give it a unified feel.

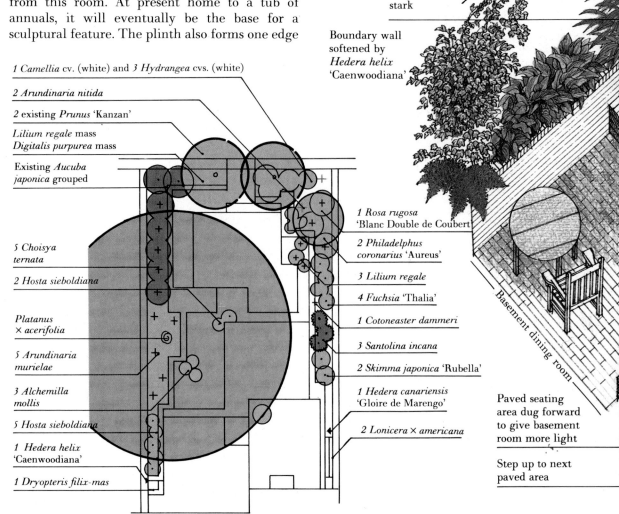

Gravel planting prevents center of garden looking stark

Boundary wall softened by *Hedera helix* 'Caenwoodiana'

1 *Camellia* cv. (white) and 3 *Hydrangea* cvs. (white)

2 *Arundinaria nitida*

2 existing *Prunus* 'Kanzan'

Lilium regale mass
Digitalis purpurea mass

Existing *Aucuba japonica* grouped

5 *Choisya ternata*

2 *Hosta sieboldiana*

Platanus × *acerifolia*

5 *Arundinaria murielae*

3 *Alchemilla mollis*

5 *Hosta sieboldiana*

1 *Hedera helix* 'Caenwoodiana'

1 *Dryopteris filix-mas*

1 *Rosa rugosa* 'Blanc Double de Coubert'

2 *Philadelphus coronarius* 'Aureus'

3 *Lilium regale*

4 *Fuchsia* 'Thalia'

1 *Cotoneaster dammeri*

3 *Santolina incana*

2 *Skimma japonica* 'Rubella'

1 *Hedera canariensis* 'Gloire de Marengo'

2 *Lonicera* × *americana*

Basement dining room

Paved seating area dug forward to give basement room more light

Step up to next paved area

Built-in bench
forms part of
garden's overall
pattern

Shade-tolerant
planting includes
Aucuba japonica

Bowl of annuals
on brick plinth to
be replaced by a
sculpture

Teak table and
chairs match

Door leading to
garage

Retaining
wall/casual
seating

Room for relaxing (below)
*The simply-shaped seating
area is couched with greenery.
The pastel impatiens in the pot
add a delicate touch.*

Fitting for subtle
evening lighting

FAMILY SPACE

When I first saw this garden it consisted of a border-edged rectangle of worn grass. The owners, who had already planned to have a dining room extension built to the back of their nineteenth-century house, decided that it would be practical to transform the garden at the same time.

Their aim was to create a space that would be enjoyed by their children as much as themselves. In addition to a paved area for having meals, they wanted a hard surface for a bench outside their studio/workshop at the end of the garden and a small sandpit and a soft area where the children could play. In including all these elements the design of the garden began to evolve like a series of small rooms.

Room for the children

In general I am in favor of gravel, rather than grass, in gardens this size, for small areas of grass often look rather depressing, particularly in the winter when they become dull and covered in muddy wormcasts. However, gravel is not a safe or pleasant medium for children to play on, so I included a small brick-edged lawn which fits neatly between the paved areas, rather like a Persian carpet on a tiled floor.

I loosened the regularity of the rectangular site by turning the series of small "rooms" on to a diagonal axis. The zig-zag shapes this creates are accentuated by brick edging. The large raised bed helps rationalize the slope of the garden from right to left (looking away from the house).

Pots and jars (above) *A cluster of pots lies across from an old stone jar.*

The new dining room (right) *Lush planting gives an air of privacy.*

Slight changes in level between the different areas increase the ground-pattern interest. A shallow step leads from the terrace nearest the house down to the lawn, from which another leads up to the paved area near the studio/workshop.

Inevitably water collects at the lowest point of the garden, in this case the lawn. The turf and its 25cm (10in) of topsoil over gravel forms a porous mat, through which water percolates to a rubble reservoir about 50cm (20 in) deep. From here it slowly disperses into the surrounding subsoil.

Personal touches

Much of the charm of this garden is its lived-in look, which comes from the collection of bric-a-brac brought back by the family from trips to the seaside and outings to country junk shops. Dotted around the garden is an assortment of old chimney-pots which have been filled with plants, old terracotta pots and cream pots (bored for drainage), stone jars, and pebbles and boulders collected from favorite holiday haunts.

Planting

Since the garden backs on to neighboring gardens on two sides, and is overlooked by a row of tall town houses on the third, this lush planting is aimed at giving the garden privacy and so includes a lot of climbers.

Different varieties of climbing ivy clothe the two side walls and the trellis that gives them extra height. Scented *Lonicera periclymenum* covers the garden's end wall.

Evergreens, including bamboos and *Euonymus fortunei* make a bold sculptural backdrop to a mass of colorful annuals and perennials, such as pink and white astilbes, purple loosestrife, and the yellow of creeping buttercups. Hydrangeas and assorted ferns grow happily in the shadiest corners. Herbs, geraniums, and small-leaved ivies grow in the clusters of pots around the garden.

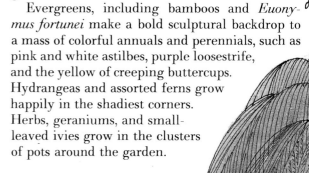

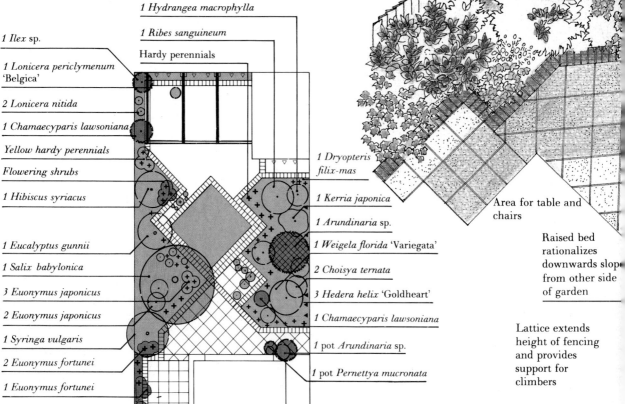

Old chimney pot planted with ivy (*Hedera* sp.)

1 *Hydrangea macrophylla*

1 *Ilex* sp.

1 *Ribes sanguineum*

Hardy perennials

1 *Lonicera periclymenum* 'Belgica'

2 *Lonicera nitida*

1 *Chamaecyparis lawsoniana*

Yellow hardy perennials

Flowering shrubs

1 *Hibiscus syriacus*

1 *Eucalyptus gunnii*

1 *Salix babylonica*

3 *Euonymus japonicus*

2 *Euonymus japonicus*

1 *Syringa vulgaris*

2 *Euonymus fortunei*

1 *Euonymus fortunei*

1 *Arundinaria pygmaea*

1 *Hedera helix* 'Goldheart'

1 *Dryopteris filix-mas*

1 *Kerria japonica*

1 *Arundinaria* sp.

1 *Weigela florida* 'Variegata'

2 *Choisya ternata*

3 *Hedera helix* 'Goldheart'

1 *Chamaecyparis lawsoniana*

1 pot *Arundinaria* sp.

1 pot *Pernettya mucronata*

Area for table and chairs

Raised bed rationalizes downwards slope from other side of garden

Lattice extends height of fencing and provides support for climbers

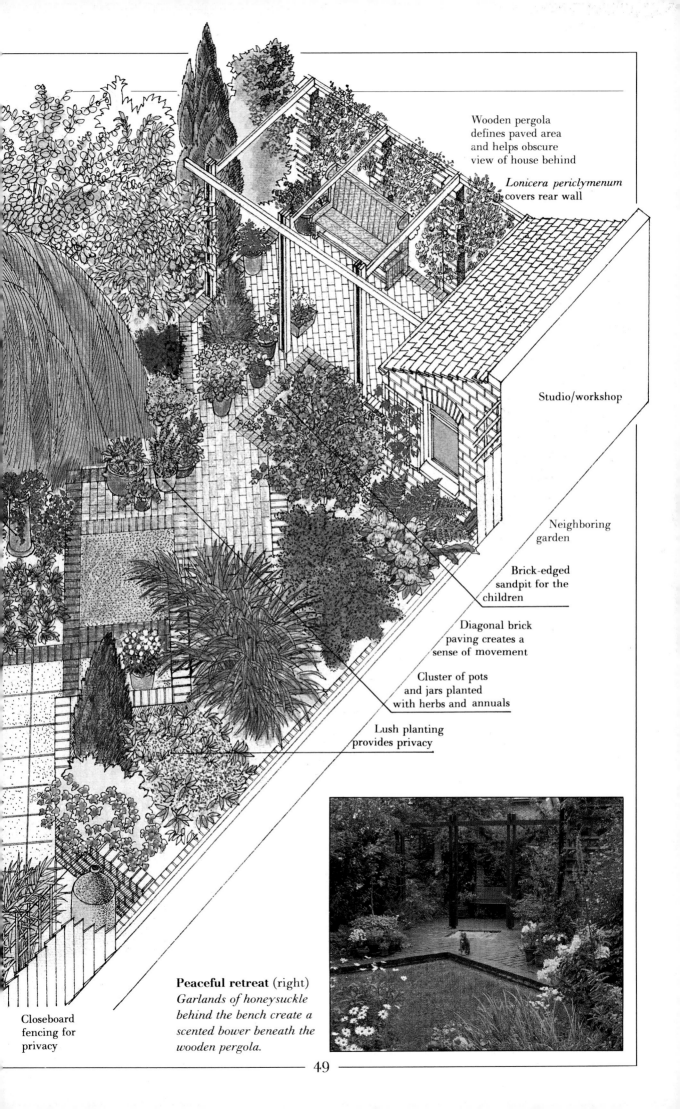

Wooden pergola
defines paved area
and helps obscure
view of house behind

Lonicera periclymenum
covers rear wall

Studio/workshop

Neighboring
garden

Brick-edged
sandpit for the
children

Diagonal brick
paving creates a
sense of movement

Cluster of pots
and jars planted
with herbs and annuals

Lush planting
provides privacy

Closeboard
fencing for
privacy

Peaceful retreat (right)
*Garlands of honeysuckle
behind the bench create a
scented bower beneath the
wooden pergola.*

URBAN RETREAT

As with many town gardens this one backs on to a counterpart site, with its house beyond, so there is little privacy and a feeling of being overlooked. In such situations the garden is a dark well, and its plants tend to reach up towards the light. To counteract this, strong foliage forms and ground-pattern are necessary to keep the eye within the site.

Transformation

Ten years ago, when I first visited the site, there was little of interest except for a 2m (6½ ft) high fence and a mature whitebeam (*Sorbus aria* 'Lutescens'). It is the position of this tree that inspired the modulated paving pattern that leads up to it, and the bench seat strengthens its visual attraction.

The crisp styling of the garden is very much in the idiom of the interior of the house – the bricks and tiles being a continuation of the flooring used in the kitchen from which it leads. Gravel makes a pleasing textural contrast with the paving, and looks neat all year round. Sculpture, on the paved area and amongst the foliage, gives the garden an extra individual touch.

Once the site was cleared, the first job was to lay the brick-edged, tiled areas. A slight change of level across the site allowed a shallow step between the sections, the line of which adds to the dynamic pull of the design towards the L-shaped wooden bench which provides casual seating in the corner of the garden.

Outside room (above)
Pig sculpture provides a whimsical diversion.

Lateral view (right)
The tiled terrace draws the eye to the seat.

The brickwork was completed by adding the brick curb, set firmly in concrete, that would contain the gravel area. The latter was completed by levelling and thoroughly consolidating a 10cm (4 in) thickness of unwashed binding gravel into the excavation, then bringing the area up to the required level by rolling in a thin layer of washed pea gravel. The finished surface is firm and easy to walk on in addition to being ideal for planting in.

Softwood lattice was made to match the dimensions of the lights in the windows that overlook the garden. Painted white and attached to the dark-stained fence, the completed panels of lattice project above the height of the existing fence, to lighten the effect.

Structures

The pergola was made by supporting simple, white-painted wooden horizontals on black-painted scaffolding poles set in concrete. The uprights are sited between the kitchen windows of the house, and the pergola's dimensions match those of a section of the adjoining neighboring house that protrudes adjacent to the site. When vine-covered in summer, the pergola shades the kitchen windows from bright morning sunshine.

A tiny wooden shed, painted white to match the paintwork of the windows, doors and pergola horizontals, was sited in the recess beyond the pergola to house a few garden tools.

Planting

The garden's planting is primarily of evergreens so that the hard edges of the garden's structure are softened the year round. The shaded site limits the choice of plants, but it includes favorites such as *Skimmia japonica* and *Fatsia japonica*.

On the lattice grow the large-leaved ivies *Hedera canariensis* 'Gloire de Marengo' and *Hedera colchica* 'Dentata Variegata', and the honeysuckles *Lonicera periclymenum* 'Serotina' and *L. periclymenum* 'Belgica'. These clothe the garden walls and add to the air of privacy.

The original planting plan included a number of perennials that have since been shaded out by evergreen growth. *Acanthus spinosus*, growing through gravel, remains in all its glory however, and additional foreground interest is provided by the fleshy leaves of *Bergenia* 'Silberlicht' and the silky, gray foliage of *Artemesia* sp. Color is now provided by terracotta pots of annuals, grouped upon the terrace, two *Hydrangea macrophylla* and by various climbers. Herbs in pots (including a bay tree and rosemary) are useful for both decorative and culinary purposes.

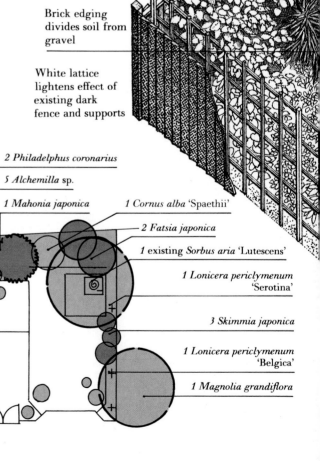

Sculpture visible from kitchen

Brick edging divides soil from gravel

White lattice lightens effect of existing dark fence and supports

1 *Hedera canariensis* 'Gloire de Marengo'

2 *Viburnum tinus*

1 existing *Magnolia* × *soulangiana*

2 *Yucca gloriosa*

Hedera colchica

2 *Bergenia* 'Silberlicht'

4 *Artemesia* sp.

3 *Escallonia* 'Iveyi'

2 *Hydrangea macrophylla*

1 *Vitis cognetiae*

1 *Hedera colchica* 'Dentata Variegata'

1 *Acanthus spinosus*

2 *Philadelphus coronarius*

5 *Alchemilla* sp.

1 *Mahonia japonica*

1 *Cornus alba* 'Spaethii'

2 *Fatsia japonica*

1 existing *Sorbus aria* 'Lutescens'

1 *Lonicera periclymenum* 'Serotina'

3 *Skimmia japonica*

1 *Lonicera periclymenum* 'Belgica'

1 *Magnolia grandiflora*

Wooden bench seat strengthens
visual pull of paving design

Sculpture visible
from reception
room

Existing tree inspired
dynamic pull of paving
design to this area

Bay-windowed
reception room

Shallow step adds
to ground-level
interest

Vitis coignetiae shades kitchen in
summer

The kitchen entrance
(below) *White-painted wooden
horizontals host an elegant
vine. Herbs (including a bay
tree) are conveniently sited
near the kitchen door.*

Kitchen
door and
windows

Pots of
annuals
for seasonal
color

Tiles match those
of the kitchen

Shed painted
white to match
other paintwork

Gravel contrasts
with paving

COUNTRY STYLE

This small, country-style garden lies cheek by jowl with the cathedral at the ancient heart of a southern English city. The owner, who had moved from a country home with a large garden, wanted a similar style of garden in which she could tend and nurture plants – her passion – albeit on a much reduced scale.

The site

Adjacent to the cottage-style house and its new extension was a terrace of random paving. From this a step (approximately 50cm (18 in) led up to an area of rough grass – very rough, in fact, for it was used as a dumping ground during alterations to the house. Beds bordered the surrounding walls.

An open area was needed, on which to stand furniture and in which to pot up plants, so the paved area adjacent to the house was retained. Visually too, it was important to keep one area free as a contrast to the spectacular array of plants with which the owner planned to fill the rest of the garden. With this in mind, the aim of the design was to create a structure that would contain and steady the mass of soft, country-style planting without dominating it, and that would blend in well with the surroundings. The looser and more relaxed the style of planting, the more important it is to have a structure both of hard materials and

A taste of the country (above) *Gentle colors and soft, country-style planting create a pleasant air of calm.*

Visual links (right) *Gravel, paving and planting all serve to bind this home to its small garden space.*

strong skeleton plants that will prevent it from becoming a muddle. By contrast, in small gardens where the owner's priority is to use the space for activities other than gardening, plants are introduced primarily to soften the strong lines of hard materials of the structural elements.

The ground-pattern

Only one of the existing border beds, and part of another were retained. All the grass was taken up and replaced with a combination of gravel, stone and brick. Brick was used to build a gentle step-up from the paved terrace adjacent to the house, to edge the beds, and make a few simple divisions within the rest of the site. A coating of pale, washed gravel was rolled into a 5cm (2 in) layer of unwashed binding gravel; this makes a textural contrast with the plants grown in it.

Old paving slabs and brick, the color of which complements that of the gravel and the house, were laid at various points throughout the gravelled area to make a path through the garden and give easy access to the plants. Their geometrical patterns contrast with the loosely-structured style of the planting.

Country-style planting

The abundance of plants and their loose arrangement form a gentle, billowing outline, typical of the country garden. Caring for a variety of plants is time-consuming, so this style of planting is suited only to those who, like the owner of this garden, are happy to devote time to them.

The harmonious, calm quality of the garden comes from the arrangement of groups of a particular plant in coherent "drifts". Dotting plants about the garden, one here and one there,

would have created a restless, ununified appearance. Great care was taken in the combination of colors. The greens, grays, and golds of foliage act as a restful backdrop to stronger, seasonal colors of the flowers.

Evergreen shrubs such as *Mahonia japonica* and the near evergreen *Viburnum × burkwoodii* give structure to the planting and provide interest during the months of winter. Their dark green foliage contrasts with that of gray plants such as *Senecio* 'Sunshine', *Hebe pinguifolia* 'Pagei' and *Lavandula angustifolia* and the purple-bronze leaves of *Ajuga reptans* 'Burgundy Glow' and the red winter stems of *Cornus alba*.

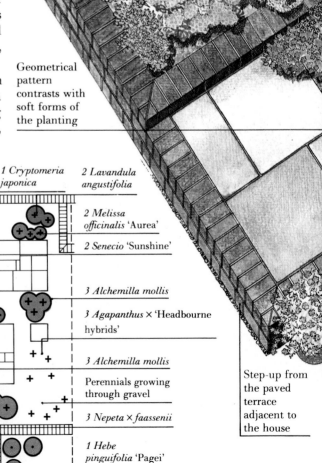

Geometrical pattern contrasts with soft forms of the planting

1 *Mahonia japonica*

1 *Cryptomeria japonica*

2 *Lavandula angustifolia*

1 *Philadelphus coronarius*

2 *Melissa officinalis* 'Aurea'

2 *Senecio* 'Sunshine'

1 *Rosa* 'Comte de Chambord'

4 *Dianthus* sp.

3 *Alchemilla mollis*

1 *Ceanothus thyrsiflorus* 'Repens'

3 *Agapanthus ×* 'Headbourne hybrids'

Anaphalis vulgaris mass

1 *Viburnum × burkwoodii*

3 *Alchemilla mollis*

Perennials growing through gravel

1 *Rosa* 'Pearl Drift'

Dianthus sp., *Aquilegia vulgaris* mass

3 *Nepeta × faassenii*

3 *Cornus alba*

1 *Hebe pinguifolia* 'Pagei'

Step-up from the paved terrace adjacent to the house

Roses for
summer scent

Brick used to
make a few
simple
divisions

Plants with a
loose form
create a gentle,
billowing
outline

The texture
of gravel
contrasts with
the plants that
grow through it

Paving slabs
make a path
through the
gravel

Softening a division
(right) *Plants in pots
soften the division
between the paved area
and the rest of the
garden.*

Deciduous shrubs including *Philadelphus coronarius* (mock orange), which has pointed oval leaves, and a variegated *Cornus alba* swell the shape of the garden when they are in leaf.

Linking colors

Traditional country garden plants, including roses, are grown together in carefully orchestrated drifts of color. In the left-hand bed, for example, catmint (*Nepeta × faassenii*), stock (*Matthiola incana*) and *Aquilegia* sp. make a billowing summer combination of gentle mauve, pink, and white. The bold evergreen foliage of *Bergenia cordifolia*, which grows amongst these, gives strength to the planting and provides interest when the flowers die away.

This gentle theme of colors is continued throughout the rest of the garden by the pink rose (*Rosa* 'Comte de Chambord'), white rose (*Rosa* 'Pearl Drift'), pink valerian (*Centranthus* sp.), more stock (*Matthiola incana*), crane's-bill (*Geranium endressii*) and lavender (*Lavandula angustifolia*).

Another theme in the color of the planting is gold. On the right-hand side of the garden grows golden balm (*Melissa officinalis* 'Aurea') and golden marjoram (*Origanum onites* 'Aureum') grows amongst lady's mantle (*Alchemilla mollis*).

The planting is as pleasing when looked down upon from the upper rooms of the house, as at

View from above *It is just as important that your garden looks attractive from the rooms above it as those at ground level – here paving and gravel give definition to the softly-formed planting.*

ground level. The colors of the plants contrast with the colors of the hard materials used and their soft forms contrast with the crunchy texture of the gravel and the smooth stone slabs. Not trying to incorporate a tiny patch of turf has allowed the garden's plants to assume a luxuriance that belies the small site.

Country-garden scent

One of the great attractions of the country garden is its scent. Here, roses give a sweet summer aroma, along with the delicious orange-scented blossoms of *Philadelphus coronarius*. These are supplemented by the herb-garden scents of catmint, lavender, balm and marjoram. The lily of the valley-fragranced blossoms of *Mahonia japonica* scent the garden from early to mid-spring The country fragrance of the garden can be enjoyed from inside too, for a climbing rose surrounds the doors and windows and catmint grows beside the house.

Butterflies and bees, attracted by the fragrant and colorful plants, add to the pleasantly countrified atmosphere of the garden.

DESIGN

Putting pen to paper and planning the layout
of your small space will enable you to get the
most from it, both visually and physically.

A step-by-step guide shows how to design your
space and how to exploit color, shape
and "special effects", while the Special Design
Cases that follow contain ideas and inspiration
on how to transform all manner of spaces
from basement yard to window-ledge.

CREATIVE PLANNING

You may find the thought of designing something, not least a garden, daunting, seeing it as the sole preserve of those "in the know" – some amorphous body of esthetes. Yet each time you decide how to arrange some ornaments on a shelf or where to position a sofa you are influenced by the basic principles of design: practical considerations such as ease of cleaning or the location of a light, as well as esthetic ones, such as the appearance of an object's shape, texture, and color in relation to surrounding objects and surfaces.

In the same way as you arrange objects in a room to make a pleasing yet functional composition, you can arrange the elements of a small garden, counterpoising an area of paving, for instance, with one of water, gravel, and planting. Good design will give you maximum pleasure from your small space, for the closer the bond between the different elements in it and its surroundings, the larger it will appear.

The basic techniques of design are explained on the next six pages, and the use of color, shape, and special effects on the following six. With all this under your belt and some ideas from the Special Design Cases you can go on to tackle the design of your own space, however small, and whatever its location.

Wall design (above)
Even if all you have to look at is a wall, creative design can produce a spectacular effect.

A sense of space (right)
Good design can suggest surprising spaciousness in a traditional, though limited site.

THE DESIGN PROCESS

The design process consists of five basic stages: assessment (of the site and your requirements), measuring-up, drawing to scale, evolving a pattern, and translating your pattern into areas of structure and planting. The design of a small town garden is taken as an example and illustrated on this and the following five pages.

Assessing the site

First, look carefully at your site, ask yourself plenty of questions and note any problems. For instance, is it overshadowed by neighboring buildings or a tall tree? Which, if any areas get the sun? Are there any eyesores you would like to disguise? Then ask yourself how you want to use the space. Do you enjoy gardening and want to devote most of the space to plants? Or do you want an area that requires minimum maintenance? Would you like to be able to use the space for parties, or do you need a play area for children?

The design brief

The small garden illustrated here lies at the rear of a terraced house and slopes gently towards a garage. The site was grassed over and dominated by a large oil tank. Both the ground-floor rooms open out into the garden and it can be seen from the rooms above. The owner wanted a garden that needed little maintenance, a clear route to the garage and an area in which to sit near the kitchen; the oil tank had to remain, so needed to be

Utilizing space *Planning your garden will enable you to make the most effective use of space. Here, two paved areas lead to a raised pool, whose wall can be used as seating and to stand pots on.*

disguised. She had a bird bath in her previous garden and now wanted a pool that would attract birds. A look at the plants in the neighboring garden confirmed that the soil was alkaline.

Measuring-up

First, draw an outline sketch of the site on which to note your measurements. Then measure across the width of the garden wall of your house, including any adjacent structures, and then measure the length of your site at an angle of 90 degrees from each side of this. If the far end of the site is narrower than the house, measure back to the house from each end of the boundary facing it. Make a note of the dimensions of permanent features (such as trees, or in this case, an oil tank) and their distance from the house and boundaries, and the height of the doors and windows and their distance from one another and the boundaries.

Drawing-up

The next stage is to draw up an accurate scaled plan of your garden. Use a scale of 1:50 (one unit of measurement on your plan for every 50 in your garden), or 1:25, whichever fits on your size of paper. Using the measurements you have taken

Measuring-up (right) *Before embarking on a design make a rough sketch of the site and incorporate the measurements (width and length) of its boundaries and any existing features. Check the services (the position of existing pipes, for instance) and make a note of these and any other important practical considerations on your sketch. For this garden the measurements of the garden walls, the oil tank, windows, doors, and garage eaves were taken.*

Drawing to scale (below) *Using an architect's scale rule draw your sketch to a scale of 1:25 or 1:50 (whichever fits on your size paper). On a separate sheet draw a grid whose squares match, or are a fraction or multiple of an existing structure (usually the width of a window). The squares on this grid were based on the width of the kitchen window and door recess.*

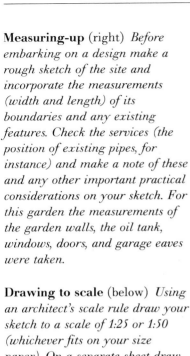

garage/store   oil

good brick wall

←——— 6M ———→
(19½ ft)

drop to house of 500mm.
(19½ in)

8·6M
(28 ft)

hot, sunny

sitting room   Kitchen

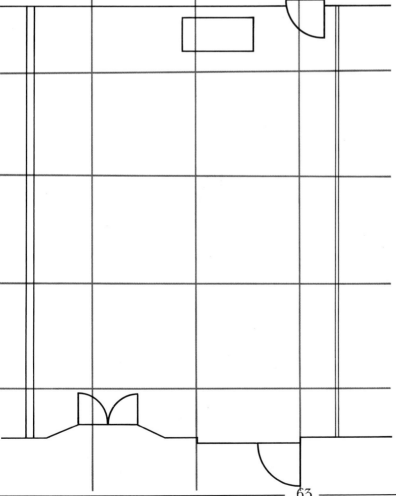

Design considerations (above) *An oil tank originally dominated the view of the garden from the house. An attempt to disguise it with trellis, served only to attract further attention to it. There was no hidden storage space, so objects like trash cans had to be kept in full view of the house.*

draw in the boundaries and the exact position of any existing features (such as steps or areas of planting) you intend to keep. Scaled rules are easily bought and will speed up this process.

Making a grid

The next stage is to devise a grid that will make any pattern you choose to fit to it, suit the proportions of your home and its garden space.

On tracing paper (so you can overlay your scaled plan and compare different patterns) draw up a series of squares that relate in size to the dimension of a permanent feature of the house or in the garden; the width of a door or height of a window, or width of a step, for instance.

Evolving a pattern *Use pieces of card (which relate in size to the grid squares) to make a pleasing pattern which broadly fulfils your requirements. The grid here is used at 90 degrees.*

In the case of the town garden illustrated here the width of the kitchen window and the door recess were used and series of squares of that size drawn up on tracing paper.

Evolving a pattern

The next stage is to evolve a pattern using your grid, and pieces of card that relate in size to the grid squares. For example, some pieces of card can be half the size, some the same size, and some double the size of the grid squares. Use the squares to create a pattern on your grid, rather like a collage. Whatever the pattern you create, it will have a proportional relationship back to the house or boundary; in this example, the pattern will have a relationship to the bay window and thus the living room which opens out on to the garden.

Try the squares at right angles to the house or at 45 degrees to it, or a combination of the two. If you want a garden pattern on the oblique (and this is a

good way of breaking up the boxiness of a small garden) turn all the cut shapes at an angle of 45 degrees. In a small space, any angle smaller than 45 degrees or larger than 90 degrees is likely to create akwardly-shaped areas that will prove difficult to deal with.

Some people consider straight lines to be unsympathetic, and would prefer to use curves, but before embarking on this remember that if the proportions are correct and the area is well planted, the straight lines will be softened by vegetation. If you want curved structures, substitute circles cut out so that their diameters equal the length of one of the sides of your grid squares, or a fraction or multiple of it.

Turning the pattern into reality *Define what form your cut-outs and the areas around them will take in reality, to make a practical "working" pattern of paved areas, planting and gravel.*

When designing a garden enclosed by walls (as many small-space gardens are) it is all too easy to be tempted to use the boundary walls as a starting off point, running a raised bed all the way round them, for instance, only to emphasize the garden's shortcomings. By using the collage method you will avoid this temptation, for your shapes will relate to the house and one another.

Relating shapes

While you are arranging your shapes bear in mind your requirements and try to imagine what form the shapes might take in reality, how they would relate to each other, and how they might look from inside at ground level and from any rooms above.

In the case of this small garden a pattern was needed that would give both terrace space and a path to the garage. A visual stop was needed when looking at the space down the length of the living room, and a screen was needed for the oil tank.

Once you have a two-dimensional design that is visually pleasing, start to take your design into the third dimension by thinking about the height or depth of the shapes. For instance, by making the squares into boxes and giving any walls within the area height, you begin to create a sort of sculpture; the same happens when you build steps or sunken areas. Color in the spaces around your cut-out shapes. When you start to select plants, it should be in the light of this sculptural effect – to create the desired bulk.

Realizing your design

Once you have a design you find visually pleasing and which seems broadly to fulfill your practical requirements, start to knock it into shape by defining exactly what form each area will take in reality. In the example illustrated on these pages the possibility of using the space between the pattern and the boundary for planting has already been considered; but what about the rest? What is to be the main feature of the garden, what should be used to screen the oil tank, which areas should be paved, and what materials should be used for the paving and the new walls?

The structure

The first step was to establish the paved areas – a terrace for a table and chairs near the house, in a sunny position, and a paved area linking the house to the garage. The site rises, so some shallow steps were incorporated as part of the pattern as well.

The next part of the process was to decide which shape was to be used as the main feature of the garden. In this case it was decided to build a pool raised by about 40cm (1½ ft). It was positioned so that it is clearly visible from the living room. The pool is backed by a free-standing brick wall containing a fountain, from which water trickles into the pool below. The same style of wall was erected beyond the pool to screen the oil tank. The walls act like the wings of a stage – both a

backdrop and a screen, and create storage space for trash cans in the far corner of the garden.

The next step was to decide what materials should be used for the terrace areas and the walls. The house and garage are both made of brick, and as the idea was to create a unified look, the new features were constructed from brick of the same color. To prevent the brickwork overwhelming the garden a central gravel area was incorporated, with square paving slabs, which act as stepping stones. The pergola was constructed of lumber, painted white to match the door and window surrounds, making a strong link between the paved area beneath it and the adjoining kitchen.

Plants and the design

When a layout such as this is newly completed, it will look extremely hard, but this effect will be beautifully softened by the introduction of plants. The styling of the plant material, its overall shape, and color and texture should relate to the style, shape, texture and color of the garden's structure and the interior of any rooms which adjoin the garden. The owner of this house was not a keen gardener, which meant plants that require little maintenance had to be chosen.

Climbers are particularly useful. Here an ivy is used to cover part of the wall that conceals the oil tank, and honeysuckle, a grape, climbing rose and clematis grow up the pergola, creating a pleasing view from the kitchen window and providing some shade. The climbers growing up the rear boundary wall make a soft textured backdrop to the angular shapes of the water feature.

The color of the planting scheme was determined by the colors used in the living room (a plum carpet and pink walls) and the color of the external brickwork. The main feature is a Japanese weeping cherry (*Prunus serrulata* 'Rosea'); this relates in scale to the boundary wall and droops over the water feature, thereby visually linking the two structures.

The original kitchen area (right) *The area immediately outside the kitchen door was originally uninviting and the view from inside was dull.*

The new kitchen area (far right) *The kitchen door now opens on to a small paved "room", defined by a pergola (the same height as the door) which makes a strong link between the garden and the house. The climbers on the pergola will mature to give a pleasant view of greenery from the window, and shade.*

The completed design *The garden has a pleasant courtyard-like quality and there is plenty of usable space. Changes of level, contrasted surfacing materials, a pergola and a water feature create a strong shape and pattern, softened by the planting. From the left-hand side of the garden the eye is led by a series of steps to the water feature and weeping cherry tree; this is counterbalanced by the wall which hides the oil tank.*

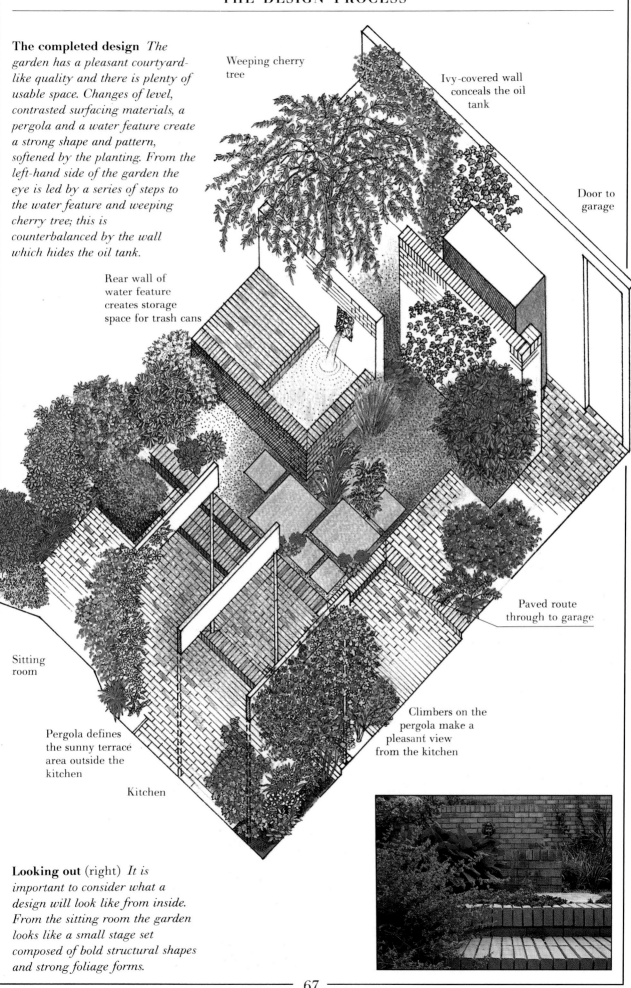

Weeping cherry tree

Ivy-covered wall conceals the oil tank

Door to garage

Rear wall of water feature creates storage space for trash cans

Paved route through to garage

Sitting room

Pergola defines the sunny terrace area outside the kitchen

Kitchen

Climbers on the pergola make a pleasant view from the kitchen

Looking out (right) *It is important to consider what a design will look like from inside. From the sitting room the garden looks like a small stage set composed of bold structural shapes and strong foliage forms.*

COLOR

Color, like sound and smell, has the power to strengthen mood. While there is no need to be specific about color as you evolve the design for your space, you should be thinking about its overall "feel" and how this can be expressed in color. The location of your site, the materials from which it is built, its aspect (whether it is sunny or not), its usage and the style of any adjoining rooms will suggest the mood.

The effects of color

Some colors are soothing and calming, others stimulating and invigorating – choose the ones that you empathize with and that reinforce the mood of your garden space. A small sunny terrace with a jacuzzi for instance, is a high-activity space which would be best suited to invigorating blues and yellows rather than purples and grays which would be too lugubrious. On the other hand too much orange and puce would be out of place in a small country-style garden, with a gentle, quiet air, which would be enhanced by colors with a calming quality, such as white, cream, and soft blues, pinks and greens.

Creating a color scheme

It is particularly important that colors work well together in a small space, for every garden element, from walls and paving to furniture and planting, will be close together and viewed as a whole, and will quite possibly be seen in conjunction with the colors inside your home. Create a color scheme for your outside space as you would a room inside, co-ordinating each part of it.

Select your plants by looking closely at a plant catalogue, or better still visit a garden center or nursery with pieces of card the same color as your structures and furnishings.

Judging the effects of light

Light affects the quality of color so bear in mind what the colors you choose will look like at different times of the day. Pale colors look pleasingly soft in gentle morning and evening light but can appear washed out in a strong noon-day sun. Conversely, colors strong enough to cope with a high noon sun can look too garish in the morning and evening. Put pieces of colored paper in sunny and shady spots and note the effects the light has on them at different times of day. Try too to visualize what the colors you choose will look like in relation to seasonal changes of color, for instance the fresh, clear shades of spring and the strong, rich shades of autumn.

Color in detail (above)
A simple combination of colors makes for a pleasing small-scale composition.

Bold statement (left)
Bold black-and-white checkered tiling is balanced by the strong colors of the planting.

Bright palette (right)
The strength of the scheme in this outside dining area is perfect in the gentle morning and evening light, but would be too garish for the noon-day sun.

SHAPE AND PATTERN

It is the shapes used in your design and the pattern they make that will set the tone of your garden's style. There are endless permutations, with at one end of the spectrum, the symmetrical arrangement of shapes that will give your space a formal, classical look, and at the other an asymmetrical arrangement of shapes that has an abstract, modern style – each suits different situations.

Shapes for small spaces

Given that many urban spaces are surrounded by structures at 90 degrees to one another, rather than flowing boundaries of fields and trees, a design of geometrical shapes with straight lines is usually most appropriate. However, circles, segments of circles, or curved lines can work, as long as they are arranged within a right-angle grid (see pp. 64–5 on using a grid for design).

In a small area the most effective designs are usually produced by using one type of shape, rather than mixing diagonals and curves for example, for the limitations of space will not usually enable you to extend such a design to its logical conclusion.

You can arrange your shapes to create a sense of movement or sense of repose. Linear shapes and patterns give a sense of movement by leading the eye. In a small space it is important that free, curved shapes have a purpose (unless the boundaries are curved) by leading the eye to a feature such as a piece of statuary within your space, or even to something outside it, such as a tree in next door's plot. Static shapes can be arranged in patterns that will hold the eye within the site; these are usually more restful and are suited to enclosed spaces where there is no focal point.

Three-dimensional shapes

Two-dimensional patterns come alive when they are taken into the third dimension by deciding on the relative height of one shape to another and selecting the materials which will "fill" them. Giving some of the shapes height will immediately give definition to others, but think also of giving some of them depth, in the form of a sunken pool or seating area, for example.

Materials

The qualitites of the materials you select to "fill" these shapes will mold the character of your garden too. You can choose from hard and soft materials, rough and smooth, light and dark, light absorbant and light reflective, in the form of brick, concrete, grass, gravel, wood and water.

Using linear shapes *Irregularly shaped spaces can be hard to deal with. The areas of paving and gravel, shown here, are fluid in their course and make a clear route between two buildings, uninterrupted by the change in level. Their bold angular shape is in style with the shapes produced by the corners of the buildings they adjoin.*

1 Circles in plan
(right) *Two overlapping circles form the basis of a simple, yet effective pattern. They relate in size to the grid squares (see pp.64–5) which in turn relate in size to the width of a bay window, so the design of the garden is strongly linked with the house.*

Simple circular design (above) *Two circles make a simple geometrical pattern in a limited space; the water-filled circle gives the design depth and the circular theme is echoed by the round table.*

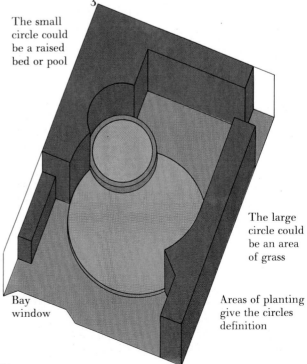

The small circle could be a raised bed or pool

The large circle could be an area of grass

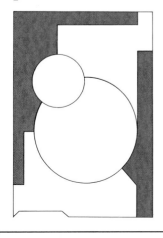

2 Defining the circles
(left) *The shaded areas that give definition to the circles could be filled with plants, and the unshaded areas paved.*

3 Sculptural circles
(right) *Bringing the areas of planting into the third dimension and raising the smaller circle gives the pattern a sculptural form.*

Bay window

Areas of planting give the circles definition

71

SPECIAL EFFECTS

There are a number of design tricks and devices, employing paint, trellis, mirrors, and the use of natural phenomena such as light and shadow, that can be used to decorate your garden and give it an exciting theatrical or dramatic flavor. Such techniques suit the character of man-made surroundings and can provide inventive ways of decorating spaces where conditions are too inhospitable for plants to grow; some can be used to create an illusion of size too.

Painted trompe l'oeil

The Renaissance Italians were the early masters of painted *trompe l'oeil*, creating lavish and apparently three-dimensional architectural scenes and rural idylls on walls both inside and out. Lively and colorful murals are often used to enliven the city landscape today – their subjects ranging from animated market scenes to window-boxes, palm trees, and bright abstract patterns.

Using reflections *A mirror, positioned behind a large piece of classical statuary, creates the illusion that another cool and leafy garden lies in an area beyond this bricked-in archway.*

Painted *trompe l'oeil* and decorative murals can be just as effective on a smaller scale. Why not paint a door to suggest another garden beyond your own, a window with a window-box (the window-box could be real) or plants and trees where the real thing cannot grow or to "thicken-up" existing vegetation? Those who use their city garden only in the evening could create a dramatic night-time scene by painting the walls midnight blue with white flowers and gray foliage (real or painted) – in combination with subtle lighting the combination would be spectacular.

Exterior grade paint should be used on garden walls. Different effects can be achieved by using matt or eggshell finishes and by perhaps using bold stencils and spray paint to create patterns as a focal point. When using paint you can afford to be brave in your design, for any real mistake can be painted over and a fresh start can be made.

Using shadow

Where the natural light is strong, position plants or architectural features where they will cast dramatic shadows on surrounding surfaces. A pergola's horizontals, for instance, can be constructed where the light will shine through them to produce a strong, geometric pattern of shadows, or plants with positive architectural form, such as *Euphorbia wulfenii*, placed in front of a plain background, such as a wall, which will display their shadows to great effect.

If the light is not strong enough to produce strong shadows, why not paint some on surrounding surfaces, using different tones of the same color to imitate shadows of varying intensity, remembering that the brighter the sun, the deeper the shadows will be.

Using mirrors

Reflections in glass and water can be used to create an illusion of size. Strategically-placed mirrors, by reflecting the area you already have, can double the size of your garden visually, or even, if correctly positioned, create the impression of an ever-receding space. Large areas of mirror are an effective way of brightening areas such as shaded basements or dark wells between city dwellings.

Always use mirrors at least 6mm ($\frac{1}{5}$ in) thick and prepare them for use out of doors by lining the back with silver foil to protect the coating and mounting them on wood; the edges should be sealed to keep out dampness. Only place mirrors in a shaded position so there is no risk of reflected sunlight singeing your plants and remember that they must be sparkling clean to be effective.

Natural shadow (left) *Strong sunlight shining through the overhead beams of a pergola produces an exciting abstract pattern of shadows in this small Mediterranean garden.*

Painted shadow (below) *Where the sun is not strong enough to create real shadows they can be imitated with different shades of paint. Here, a shadow-pattern of two tones of blue paint and the reflections of the pergola beams in a pool of water combine to create a cool-colored composition.*

Mirrors can be placed where they are quite obviously a feature in their own right, or they can be disguised to deceive the viewer, as in the photograph, left, where a mirror disguised as an arch in a boundary wall gives an impression of another garden beyond it. Another way of creating a false entrance is to place a mirror behind a wrought-iron gate, a louvered door, or black, laquered Japanese-style screen.

Mirrors can also be used to draw the attention to a special feature such as a statue or a collection of topiary. They produce an especially atmospheric effect in deeply shaded corners where they reflect the little light there is.

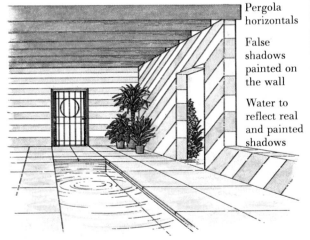

Pergola horizontals

False shadows painted on the wall

Water to reflect real and painted shadows

Reflections in water

A small pool of water, however shallow, will make your space appear larger. You can use a light-absorbent lining, such as black plastic, which will make the water surface reflect the surroundings like a mirror, while creating the impression that the pool has infinite depth. Alternatively, you can use a light-reflective one, such as mirror tiles, to reflect overhanging features, such as a piece of sculpture or some eye-catching plants, and increase the amount of light in your garden. A mirror alongside, to reflect the reflections in the water, will increase the visual excitement further and give your space an impression of size.

Using paint (left) *Painted* trompe l'oeil, *like this charming scene which surrounds a lift shaft in a French flower market, or a simple abstract mural, can be used to transform the smallest and dingiest of walled spaces.*

BASEMENTS

Below-ground-level-living is becoming more and more common as large, old houses are divided into smaller units. The outside area left to basement homes often consists of a small space wedged between street level and front door, or a small sunken backyard. Towered over by the walls of adjacent buildings, they tend to be gloomy and damp, but there are many ways of making them both stylish and usable.

Improving conditions
Basement areas are often damp. Repairing or installing a damp-proof course in surrounding walls will ensure garden drainage and moisture never infiltrates inside. Surface water should be channelled into a storm water system, if possible. If your basement area has been excavated to a level where there is nothing but impervious subsoil, it is essential to provide adequate drainage for gardening. Before planting, the subsoil should be excavated to a depth of 1m (3 ft) and filled with a layer of loose

Basement entrance **The shape and scale of large plants with bold foliage complement the character of this basement. Small, delicate plants would have been dwarfed by the surrounding structures.**

material (such as broken brick or stone), followed by a layer of soil for the plants.

Structural changes
Basement areas can be transformed by building in a series of slightly raised "pads". Two or three of these arranged in an overlapping pattern will create a sense of movement which will prevent the eye from wandering up surrounding walls and out of the site. Series of gentle level changes can also be used to great effect in areas between street level and a small basement entrance, as shown in the design solutions on the right-hand page.

Color is the obvious way of bringing interest to a basement area and to brighten it up if it is shady. Paint the walls, perhaps

with a *trompe l'oeil*, or experiment with mirrors to add visual excitement and make the area appear larger (see pp.72–3).

Visual anchors
Providing a feature to anchor the eye within your site will prevent it from being dominated by surrounding buildings. Whether you choose a piece of furniture, a plant, or a piece of sculpture, keep its scale *large* in relation to the size of the space, for tiny delicate features will look insignificant and provide no anchor at all.

Colored planting
Single-color planting schemes, using light tones of gold and silver, for instance, are an effective way of bringing life to a basement yard.

Alternatively, you might like to rely on the shape and texture of foliage. Be wary of what you plant directly alongside a high wall, for tall plants will lean inwards to reach the light. A list of plants suitable for growing in shade appears on pages 208–9.

Room for design – basement
(below) *This basement consists of a sunken area lying between the street and a basement entrance. Steep steps lead down from street level to the small paved area, which is surrounded by walls.*

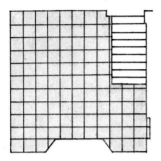

Design solution – version two
(below) *Storage is often a problem in small gardens. Here, a storage space has been included as an integral part of the design. It acts as a visual pivot for the series of paved level changes and provides the area near the house with a measure of privacy.*

Design solution – version one
The original basement area has been transformed by replacing the original steep flight of steps with a series of gentle changes in level which make a gradual transition to street level. The shapes of the stepped levels, built-in storage space and areas of planting, and

the pattern of the paving all provide a strong visual anchor which prevents the eye from wandering up the surrounding walls or straight through the site to street level. A large piece of sculpture acts as a central focal point; areas of planting echo the shapes of the design.

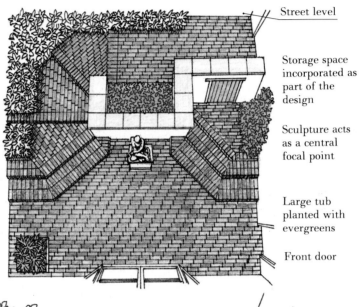

Street level

Storage space incorporated as part of the design

Sculpture acts as a central focal point

Large tub planted with evergreens

Front door

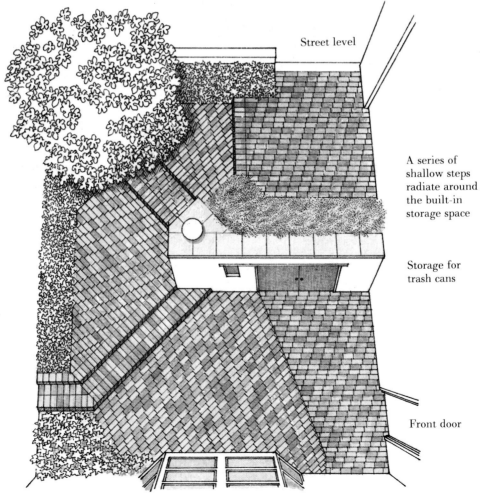

Street level

A series of shallow steps radiate around the built-in storage space

Storage for trash cans

Front door

NARROW SPACES

Narrow passageways and side entrances tend to be shady, drafty, and generally unappealing. More often than not they become home to an untidy group of trash cans and old household bits and pieces. However, with the help of a few structural alterations and the introduction of plants as a soft overlay they can be transformed into spaces that are pleasant to walk through and look at, both from inside and the street.

Architectural solutions

Long narrow spaces draw the eye through them, often to an ugly endpoint – a delapidated fence, or run-down building. The directional pull of a passageway can be used to positive effect to draw attention to an eye-catching feature at the end of it – a dramatic piece of sculpture, a large urn on a plinth or *trompe l'oeil* painted on the wall at the bottom of the passage are all suitable for this.

Alternatively, the area can be given an impression of breadth by the arrangement of features or ground surface materials which draw the eye from side to side. Planters built across the passageway, or areas of paving across gravel will have this effect; for a stronger effect still, use a combination of both.

Screens and pergolas

A screen can be used to break up the view down a passageway by creating a frame for various areas of interest. If infilled with a solid material (glass for a view through, or painted wood to block an ugly view) it will also block uncomfortable drafts.

Tall buildings or boundary walls towering on either side of a passageway produce an unpleasant "chasm" effect which can be reduced by erecting pergola horizontals across the area. (See p.197 for construction details.) Hanging baskets can be attached to the beams. Solid screens made of

Using directional pull (above)
The length of the space has been emphasized by a linear arrangement of gravel and planting that leads the eye towards a statue.

brick, concrete or timber, projecting like buttresses from the side walls, will also help reduce the effect and can be softened by growing climbers along them.

A soft overlay

Having used architectural solutions to solve the basic visual shortcomings of the space, use plants to soften the hard outlines of most of its structural elements.

Containers or planters are indispensable, for most plants can be grown in them and they save on importing quantities of soil, where none already exists. As shade and draft do not make for ideal growing conditions, you may need to choose plants which are tough. For year-round shape select a handsome evergreen shrub, perhaps from *Pyracantha* spp. (which will tolerate full shade) or *Fatsia japonica* (which tolerates semi-shade). Climbers can be used to break up large areas of wall. *Parthenocissus* spp. can withstand drafts and grow in semi-shade and *Hedera* spp. survive in shade.

Room for design – (below) *This uninviting side entrance is transformed in three different ways in the design solutions on this page. Rather than resting in the area the eye is drawn straight through and out of it by the right-hand wall. The entrance is also drafty – wind funnels through the passageway from the viewpoint.*

Design solution – version one (left) *Three brick planters built across the passageway create a sense of movement that detracts attention from the length and narrowness of the area by leading the eye, rhythmically, from side to side. Evergreen shrubs in the planters act as a windbreak and create screened storage spaces.*

Timber screen with glass panels provides shelter

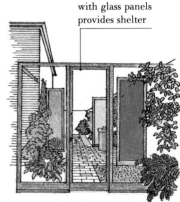

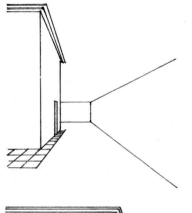

Design solution – version two (right) *A wooden screen, infilled with sheets of glass, shelters the passageway from the wind without blocking out the light. (To completely obscure an unwanted view use brightly painted wooden panels instead of glass.) Painted brick screens echo the shape of the glass panels and a T-shaped area of paving creates a sense of breadth.*

Boldly-arranged plant groupings disguise the boundary wall

Design solution – version three (left) *Three different surface materials have been used to break up the narrow area and give it an illusion of size. Brick paving leads the eye across the foreground to an area of gravel, and down to an area of grass.*

STEPS

Though steps hardly conform to most people's idea of a garden they provide the frustrated urban gardener with a valuable space for growing plants (in pots on the steps themselves, or either side of them) and can be styled so they make a visually pleasing link with the home and its interior.

Styling steps

Basic structural repairs, such as replacing crumbling brickwork and broken treads, will not only improve the look of the steps but make them safer to use, as will attention to details, such as the addition of a stylish handrail and light fittings.

New stairways should be designed so they blend in with surrounding architecture. Use the same, or similar materials and try to echo features. A gently-curved stairway, for example, will enhance round-topped doors and arched windows.

An L-shaped return at the bottom of a stairway (see version one, opposite) will make the stairway

Step garden *This handsome flight of steps which curves gracefully around a wall fountain and pool, and encloses a paved area with two seats, is the main feature of a small garden's design.*

spacious and provide a spot for standing pots or sculpture without blocking the stairs. A turn in the stairway creates an added sense of movement and the area beneath it can be used for storage (see version three, opposite).

Plants for steps

Plants alongside steps should have bold, architectural shape so that they balance the steps' strong structural form. Evergreen shrubs are ideal, for they provide shape and interest all year round. Handrails and adjacent walls can be decorated with climbers, and colorful annuals grown in pots on the steps themselves (take care not to impede the pathway). If you live on a busy roadway choose plants that are resistant to polluted air (see pp.211–2).

Room for design – before (below) *This old, run-down flight of steps, which leads up from street level to a city home, is transformed into an inviting entrance "garden" in the three design solutions shown on the opposite page. The steps not only look bare and uninviting but are unsafe because of the worn and cracked treads.*

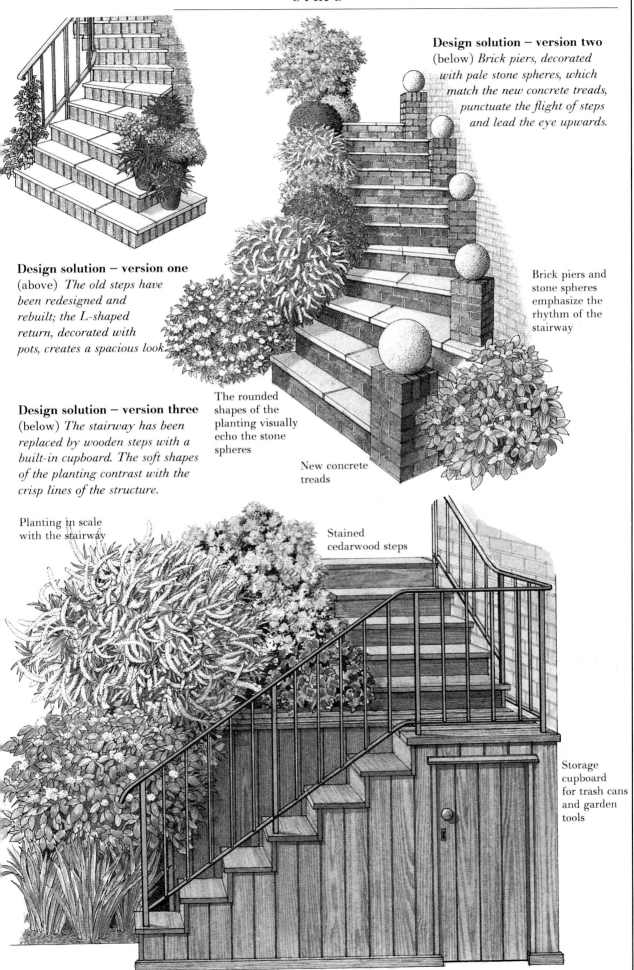

Design solution – version two
(below) *Brick piers, decorated with pale stone spheres, which match the new concrete treads, punctuate the flight of steps and lead the eye upwards.*

Brick piers and stone spheres emphasize the rhythm of the stairway

Design solution – version one
(above) *The old steps have been redesigned and rebuilt; the L-shaped return, decorated with pots, creates a spacious look.*

The rounded shapes of the planting visually echo the stone spheres

New concrete treads

Design solution – version three
(below) *The stairway has been replaced by wooden steps with a built-in cupboard. The soft shapes of the planting contrast with the crisp lines of the structure.*

Planting in scale with the stairway

Stained cedarwood steps

Storage cupboard for trash cans and garden tools

ROOF-SPACES

For town- and city-dwellers, roof-tops are particularly valuable areas that can be transformed into congenial places on which to sunbathe, entertain, eat outside, and on which children can play (providing that there are adequate safety barriers).

Creating a roof-top room

Try to create a room-like atmosphere so that you feel you are sitting *in* the roof-space as you would a room, rather than perched *on* it, for the enormity of the sky overhead and a view stretching into the distance can be rather overwhelming. Painting walls, replacing or covering the original roofing material with weatherproof flooring or lightweight paving, lighting for the evenings and furniture will all make a roof-space more congenial.

Planting can then be used to add a refreshing touch of greenery and color that will soften the stark lines of surrounding buildings. Because roofs are exposed to the elements, permanent planting

Cityscape (above) *Greenery makes a refreshing contrast with the city landscape beyond.*

Sitting space (left) *Planting is confined to containers at the sides of the roof, leaving maximum room for furniture.*

must be resilient (see pp.176–7 for suitable plants), or given shelter from strong winds.

A convenient water supply and regular maintenance are vital to their success because the wind has a dehydrating, foliage-burning effect and container-grown plants have a limited moisture reserve.

Always consult your landlord and/or a structural engineer before using a roof or making any structural changes to it. Heavy elements are best sited over or close to direct structural support – usually the edge of the roof-space.

Room for design – roof-space

(below) *The two treatments on this page show contrasted ways of transforming this unused roof-space. The roof is covered by a bitumen sealant and there is a disused chimney stack on the left-hand side. Access is through a window situated at the viewpoint – in design solution version one this is simply replaced by a door, in version two a completely new access is built into the side of the pitched slate roof, which contains a new living room.*

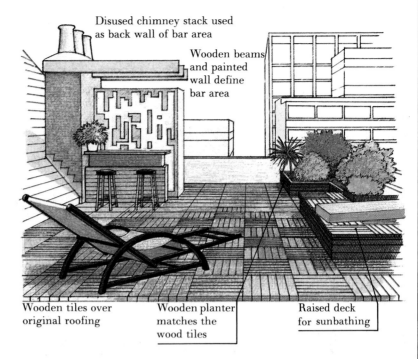

Disused chimney stack used as back wall of bar area

Wooden beams and painted wall define bar area

Wooden tiles over original roofing

Wooden planter matches the wood tiles

Raised deck for sunbathing

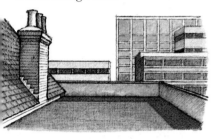

Design solution – version two

(below) *This roof-top design is more formal and less flamboyant in style than version one, so that it works as a visual extension to a new sitting room (built under the pitched roof).*

Design solution – version one

(above) *The previously ignored roof-space, shown above, left, has been transformed into a bright and informal room designed for partying and relaxing. The area in front of the disused chimney stack has been turned into a jazzy bar.*

Plan of version two

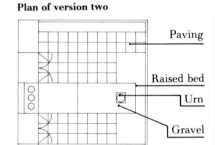

Paving

Raised bed

Urn

Gravel

Wooden beams emphasize the symmetry of the design

Trellis planted with ivy and clematis provides shelter and privacy

French doors lead to new living room built into the roof-space

Wooden rectangle with fiberglass pool links the eye with the two raised wooden beds opposite and the urn which punctuates the overall layout

Gravel contrasts with the lightweight paving

Raised bed in wood to match the sides to the doors and rectangular pool

BALCONIES

A balcony, however small, can be transformed into a valuable visual extension of the living area it adjoins, to be enjoyed all year round, and, though it may be dusty and windy, can be a pleasant place on which to tend a few plants and sit or entertain in the summer.

Styling a balcony
Using the same flooring inside and out is one of the simplest and most effective ways of integrating a balcony with an adjoining room. Standing a few pots of plants on the interior flooring will strengthen the link by bringing outside in. Use the same style of furniture you have inside on the balcony, or just take a few of your usual chairs outside (this will solve the problem of storing extra furniture) and continue your interior color scheme outside by painting walls in the same or similar shades.

Lighting your balcony artificially (either from outside or inside) will enable you to extend its use on summer evenings. But, whatever

the time of year, sympathetic lighting will enhance a balcony after dark, making it a view in its own right or providing an interesting foreground to the city lights that lie beyond.

Shade and shelter
Awnings, a large umbrella (see pp.138–9) or roller blinds like those in design solution version one, are the obvious ways to provide shade. But plants can be useful as well as decorative. Shrubs, like box, or climbers, like ivy, trained up trellis, fencing or over railings, will provide shelter from the wind and a measure of privacy, as well as obscuring unwanted views. If you have a lot of plants try to fit a water point nearby to facilitate watering. (See pp.176–7 for plants suitable for balconies.)

If you devise a scheme that involves structural changes check that you have any necessary permission and consult a structural engineer about the weight capacity of your balcony.

Cheerful color (above) *Yellow wallflowers* (Cheiranthus cheiri) *planted in pots, tubs, and hanging baskets bring exuberant color to this town balcony.*

Room for design – balcony (below) *The three design treatments on the opposite page show contrasted ways of transforming this small, city balcony into a congenial area in which to be and a stylish extension of the inside living area. The balcony space is surrounded by a low boundary wall, separated from a neighboring balcony by a glass panel, and divided from the adjoining living area by two sliding glass doors.*

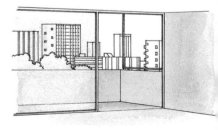

Slatted linen curtain

Matching awning and roller blinds for shade and privacy

Painted wall inside matches the awning and wall outside

Kentia palm (*Howea belmoreana*) adds to the tropical look

Wooden panel flooring blends with the overall color scheme

Wickerwork furniture used inside and outside

Design solution – version one
(above) *Strong, tropical pattern and color are used inside and out, bringing light and life to the balcony and linking it with the living room it adjoins.*

Design solution – version two
(left) *A yew hedge provides shade and privacy, and clipped box year-round sculptural interest. Pots of bulbs and annuals bring a splash of seasonal color.*

Design solution – version three
(right) *A wall partially encloses the front of the balcony and creates two "windows". Louvered screens on runners can be slid from side to side to give different views of the balcony and skyline, creating dramatic effects, rather like those of a stage set.*

WINDOWS

Windows make an excellent focus for decoration with paint, trellis-work, plants and containers, and have a special importance for those for whom they are the only gardening space. Planning and planting a window-box can be highly satisfying when the effect works!

Window decoration

Choose plants and containers that suit the style of your window space by looking at the color of your window-frame, its surround, and the color scheme of the room inside. Ask yourself whether you want your arrangement to look most effective from outside (like that shown in version three) or inside (like that in version two) and arrange plants in containers that can be seen from inside so they look pleasing when looking out through the window.

If you have no windowsill or your window opens outwards hang window-boxes beneath your window, or pots around it. Alternatively climbers can be grown from ground-level and trained around a window. If your window is at street level and you want a measure of privacy use plants in window-boxes, or grow them from ground level to screen your room from passers-by.

Flamboyant scheme (above) *A spectacular arrangement of colorful mixed pelargoniums complements this sunlit louvered window.*

Leafy screen (left) *Bamboos (*Arundinaria sp.*) planted out in a shaded window-box, create a soft, leafy screen which provides a ground-level room with privacy from passers-by without the effect of blocking out too much daylight.*

Room for design – before
(below) *Different styles of window have different practical and visual requirements. The three different types of window illustrated below are each decorated in contrasted styles in the design solutions on this page, using a simple and effective combination of plants, containers, trelliswork and paint. Before embarking on a window scheme it is important to decide whether you want it to have most impact*

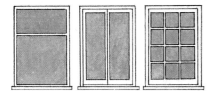

when looked at from the street, or from inside (you may decide to decorate the internal window surround).

Design solution – version one
(above) *A hanging basket provides a refreshing view of greenery out through an apartment-block window which has no sill on which to rest containers. The basket hangs from strong wire attached to a metal pin in the wall above the window.*

Design solution – version two
(above) *A lattice panel forms part of the interior decor and blends in with the scheme of crisp, country colors and the sheaf of corn.*

Design solution – version three
(above) *Trellis (like that used above) attached outside a window supports yellow climbing roses.*

Dark blue window frame contrasts with pale blue wall

Terracotta flower pots in metal hoops

Pots should be taken inside when watered to prevent drips falling on passers by

Design solution – version five
(above) *Herbs grow in a window-box that hangs below an outward-opening window.*

Design solution – version four
(above) *A Mediterranean-style arrangement of terracotta pots, filled with white, yellow, and orange begonias and purple basil makes a colorful contrast with* *the dark blue window-frame and pale blue walls. The pots around the window make a spectacular display from the street and those on the windowsill can be enjoyed from inside.*

STORAGE SPACE

One problem in many small gardens is the lack of storage space — not only for the usual trash cans, but for household bits and pieces, children's toys, and for compost, flower pots and gardening tools.

In a large garden such objects can usually be kept in a shed or discreetly hidden in a little-used space. In a small garden, however, where a free-standing garden shed will use up too much space, they are likely to be on permanent view unless some other type of provision for storage is made.

Built-in storage

One solution is to build in a storage space that is an integral part of the design of your garden. Use brick, wood or whatever material blends in with other structures in your garden. Good use can be made of awkward corners by building cupboards tailored to fit neatly into the space and designed to meet your exact requirements. The three designs on the right show ways of incorporating

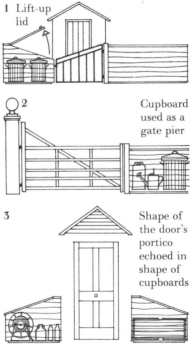

1 Lift-up lid

2 Cupboard used as a gate pier

3 Shape of the door's portico echoed in shape of cupboards

Design solutions *Three stylish designs for built-in storage.*
1 *A cupboard with a lift-up lid makes for easy day-to-day use.*
2 *A storage cupboard designed as an extension to a gate.*
3 *Two angular cupboards that echo the style of a door.*

Built-in storage space (above)
Timber cupboards, painted to match a clapboarded house, provide unobtrusive storage.

storage spaces into an entrance area. As part of the design of a door or gate, such practical solutions can be stylish features.

Cupboards which are to be used for storing rubbish must be accessible and easy to clean. Items that are to be stored on a more long-term basis can be kept in less accessible places. A hollow brick bench with a removable wooden surface is ideal.

Other solutions

An openwork screen, such as trellis clothed with climbers, or a solid one, such as closely-lashed bamboo, can be used to divide off a small area for trash cans or for a compost heap. Hedging plants make equally effective screens — make sure you choose an evergreen, otherwise you will find yourself with only a seasonal, rather than a permanent screen.

STRUCTURE

The materials from which your space is
constructed, the way in which they are
arranged, and the style of its furnishings all
mould its character.

As well as looking at the practical and visual
pros and cons of different materials and styles
of construction, there are ideas on how to
integrate "inherited" structures into your
design and how to choose furnishings, such as
pots and lighting, which will complement
the whole.

GARDEN HARDWARE

The structure of a small-space garden can be one of the most exciting things about it, and may well need to be if, as is often the case, its size and location make scope for planting restricted or non-existent. The shapes of various surfaces, gravel and paving for instance, and water and walls, and the characteristics of the materials from which they are made will give your garden permanent pattern, color and texture. Even for those primarily interested in horticulture the structure is important, for just a collection of plants will become a nondescript mess if it is not contained and offset by a strong permanent structure. A structure can be the main focus of interest in its own right, like the wooden steps shown below, or it can work together with plants to create a perfect balance of hard and soft materials, like the garden shown on the right-hand page.

It is the structure that binds the garden, visually and physically, with its site – linking the house to the garden and the garden to the surround. The closer the link between a small space and its immediate surroundings (these often being the house and its interior) the larger that space will appear.

People need structure in their garden space too to provide shelter and privacy, a practical surfacing on which to walk, stand furniture, and so on. A "good" structure will suit your needs as much as those of the plants and other "furnishings" in it.

Sculptural structure
(above) *These wooden steps are an arresting feature in their own right.*

Structure and planting
(right) *A perfect balance of hard structure and soft plant forms.*

WALLS

One of the reasons why the traditional English country walled garden is a fascinating model for so many small-space gardeners is because their own site is hemmed in by the walls of surrounding buildings, several stories high, and of neighboring gardens. But country garden solutions are probably not the way to avoid that uncomfortable claustrophobic feeling common in town gardens.

Sometimes it is necessary to build a new boundary wall or replace an old crumbling one, but more often we have to deal with the effect that "inherited" walls have on our small-garden space.

The higher the boundary walls, the stronger the inclination to look up and out of the well they create, and the greater the need to counteract this tendency in your design. This can be done by building in a strong visual feature or features (in scale with the walls) that will hold the eye in the site, or by decorating the walls (various ways of doing this are shown on pp.94–5).

Resist the temptation to work on a small scale just because you are dealing with a small space. In order for features to command attention they must be in scale with the surrounding walls. Take, for example, a small garden surrounded by a 2m (6½ ft) wall. If this measurement is used within the space, a 2 × 2m (6½ × 6½ ft) mass of planting and a paved area, or children's sandpit for example, you will start to integrate the scale of the walls with that of the space enclosed and relieve the tight

Walled garden (right) *The painted concrete walls that enclose this garden have been given a crisp, post-modern update by pieces of wooden trellis.*

Wall collage (above) *Cedarwood offcuts have been used to create an abstract collage in a garden by Garret Eckbow. Such techniques are an effective way of decorating bland areas of wall.*

Dramatic screen (left) *The height and juxtaposition of these concrete walls (cast in situ) create visual tension and drama and provide the garden with shelter and privacy without making it appear boxed in.*

"banding" effect that walls can have. A design build-up based on these principles is illustrated in the series of drawings below.

The style of your internal, sculptural build-up will depend on the style of your house, and the materials from which this and the garden walls are made. Features, such as a built-in bench or a small pool, built in the same material as the surrounding walls and your home will give the garden a satisfying integrated look.

Using retaining walls

Regard the elevation of the boundary walls as the back of a stage set and use low retaining walls to add interest to the set and lead the eye from the top of the boundary walls to ground level.

Providing that the boundary walls are structurally sound, the area between them and the low retaining walls can be backfilled with drainage material and earth and used for planting. Do not though, in a small space, construct retaining walls all round the perimeter of existing high walls, for this will reinforce the tight "banding" effect of the original walls, and make them appear even more dominating. Instead, break up the areas of retaining wall and use their dimensions to bring shape and pattern to the garden.

It is important that walls built to retain the weight of earth are strong (the construction details of a low retaining wall are shown on p.194) and that they are damp-proofed. Attention to such matters will save you both time and money later.

Design for a walled garden
This build-up, from plan to three-dimensional realization, shows how you can work in scale with surrounding walls to create a design that links the ground and walls together. This will prevent the walls from dominating the space and creating an uncomfortable boxed-in feeling. Two squares and a rectangle are worked into an interlocking pattern (counterposed by a sculptural feature in scale with the rear wall) that provides plenty of visual interest and holds the eye firmly within the site.

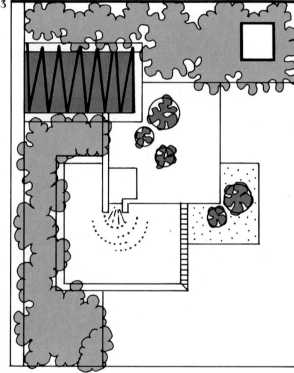

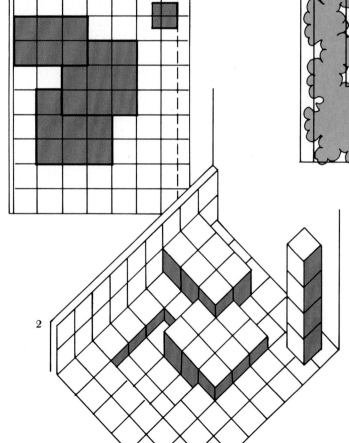

1 *Evolve a proportionate design in which the shapes relate in scale to the enclosed space.*
2 *Build up the design by giving the shapes height, thus making a three-dimensional composition.*
3 *Make a plan, deciding what form you want each of the areas to take in reality.*
4 *In the three-dimensional realization of the design, areas of paving, gravel, water and planting create a strong sculptural effect that holds the eye within the site.*

Low walls can also be used to support paved terraces or to form a series of stepped levels. The arrangements of these should suit the shape of your garden space and they should be in style with the architecture of adjoining buildings. It may be that a classical, symmetrical arrangement suits the proportions of your garden and the style of your home or alternatively the angular shape formed by the corner of your house within the yard calls for an asymmetric arrangement (see pp.70–1 on design and shape).

Maintaining walls

It is very important to look after walls, particularly old walls with weak mortar, which the damp and aerial roots of climbing plants may cause to crumble. Damp walls need to be treated before they become unsound. Call on expert advice to locate the source of the damp; it may be that a neighbor has built up the level of earth above the damp-proof course, or that the wall has no damp-proof course at all.

Outside walls can be decorated in a similar manner to inside walls – they can be painted, tiled, hung with ceramics and shelves, and so on. Such techniques are a good way of brightening up a small-space garden while leaving maximum ground space for use, and of breaking up solid areas of surrounding wall.

In warm climates, walls are often colorfully painted to relieve the sun's glare, while in duller climes the idea is to relieve the gloom. You might

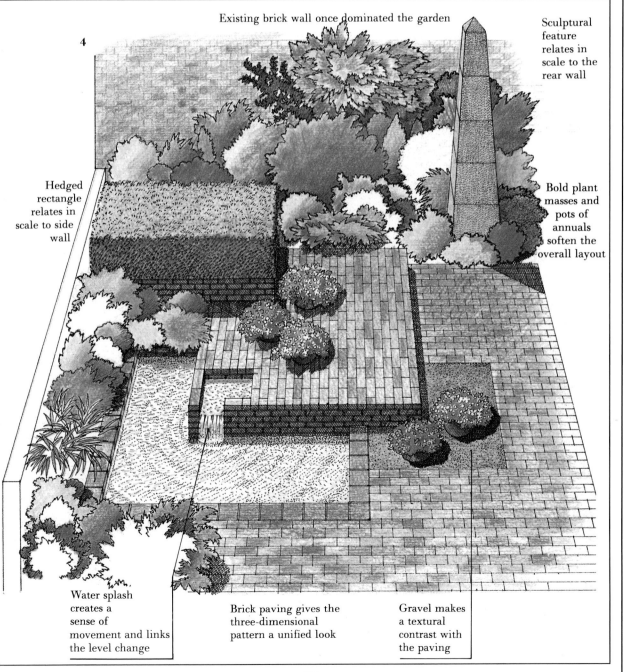

4

Existing brick wall once dominated the garden

Sculptural feature relates in scale to the rear wall

Hedged rectangle relates in scale to side wall

Bold plant masses and pots of annuals soften the overall layout

Water splash creates a sense of movement and links the level change

Brick paving gives the three-dimensional pattern a unified look

Gravel makes a textural contrast with the paving

think pure white is a good idea in drab conditions but it has a tendency to turn to muddy gray when wet. Boundary walls painted in different colors or in several tones of the same color will enliven a small enclosed space and counteract its oppressiveness. Abstract patterns of shape and color or a realistic scene can be painted on walls too, or false shadows that will create interesting effects when overlapped by real ones (see pp.72–3 on the use of "special effects").

Shelves and panels

Collections of pots, pebbles and shells can be arranged on shelves attached to outside walls. Ensure first that the wall is strong enough to support the weight of the shelves and the objects on them. Roof-garden owners can reduce the amount of weight on the roof itself by standing container-grown plants and decorative objects on shelves attached to the main structural walls of the building it adjoins.

Source of inspiration *A wall by Gaudi made up of brightly-colored broken tiles. We use patterned tiles on inside walls so why not decorate some of the walls of your outside room in a similar manner?*

Sculptural panels are an effective way of decorating walls too. An arrangement that will bring textural interest to a bland wall can be made from painted or stained wood off-cuts mounted on a wooden panel.

Climbers, or plants that can be trailed over the top of a wall are an ideal way of bringing color and textural interest to a bare wall, and will save you occupying valuable ground space with plants. (See pp.152–5 for plants that grow vertically.)

Using climbers

Dramatic combinations can be made by painting a wall in one color and training a climber in a contrasting color over it. Panels of trellis, either covered with climbers, or perhaps painted, can be used to disguise ugly walls.

Over a long period of time self-clinging climbers like ivy will begin to erode the coursing of old walls built with lime mortar. However, modern cement mortar is more resilient, and climbers will have no appreciably adverse effects. Climbers, particularly evergreens, grown against any type of wall should be clipped well back, in order to prevent dead foliage, or birds' nests collecting, for these will cause damp to penetrate the structure.

FOCUS ON WALLS

While we happily decorate the walls inside our homes with colorful paint, hang wall panels, shelves, and collections of plates on them and stand pieces of sculptural interest in front of them, we shy away from doing the same sort of thing outside. Using similar techniques on outside walls, where there is the added bonus of being able to enjoy the color and texture of plants that will climb up them or trail over them, will not only help create a congenial room-like atmosphere but will also alleviate the feeling of constriction so common in small spaces surrounded by high walls. Walls can be treated like an empty canvas and decorated so they become a focus of interest in their own right. Alternatively they can be used as a backdrop to foreground features.

Using the wall as a backdrop *This sand-colored wall acts as a simple backdrop for an African mural and tones with its natural colors of sunburned earth and stone. The composition is enhanced by the spiky, fronded leaves of a palm* (Cycas revoluta) *which casts dramatic shadows across the wall and mural.*

Wall sculpture *Curved bull-nosed bricks have been used to depict the shape of a tree in this wall sculpture. Plants beneath the tree, and two metal birds resting on its "branches" complete the picture. Live birds could be encouraged to sit on the "tree" by placing clusters of nuts or bread on top of the bricks.*

Decorative ceramics *A terracotta sun creates a focal point on a cedar shingled wall. It is surrounded by terracotta pots of* Pelargonium tomentosum, *whose leaves complete the composition.*

Colorful wall planting *Plants can be used to soften the lines of walls – here lilac-colored swathes of* Ceanothus sp. *(which grows best in full sun) tumble over a painted concrete wall.*

Evergreen "clothing" *Evergreen climbers, like this ivy* (Hedera cv.), *are an ideal way of clothing garden walls, the color and texture of their foliage providing year-round interest.*

WALL CHOICES

When choosing a wall material you should think about how the color, texture, and unit size of different materials will suit the surrounding structures. Try to visualize the massed effect of a unit, for this can be startlingly different to looking at one example in isolation.

Brick is the most popular, for the enormous range of colors and textures makes it possible to find one to complement almost any setting. Their small unit size makes them ideal for use in small and awkwardly-shaped spaces where it is often necessary to build curved or complexly-shaped walls. They are also excellent for building water features, seating, and so on.

Engineering bricks, facing bricks, infill or common bricks, and secondhand bricks can be used for building walls. Engineering bricks are the hardest (throughout their structure); facing bricks are not as hard as these, but they are stronger than infill or common brick, which must be covered with mortar (rendered) for protection against frost.

Both engineering and facing brick will give a smooth, slick appearance. In contrast, secondhand or used bricks (these will be hard enough to have been reclaimed – therefore engineering or facing) have an uneven surface because they are already weathered; these lend themselves well to walls adjacent to older buildings. Facing bricks are only weather-proofed on their finished face, so the top of a brick wall should be protected with a coping.

Concrete blocks are made from a variety of aggregates, resulting in a wide range of colors and textures. They are manufactured in larger unit sizes and are cheaper than bricks, which makes a concrete wall speedier and less costly to build than a brick one (see p.194 for construction details of a blockwork wall.) Concrete can also be poured *in situ* to make a very strong wall with a smooth surface. In rural areas local stone will probably suit surrounding buildings and landscape best. Reconstituted stone has a more regular shape making it better suited to the urban environment.

Facing brick is available in many textures and colors

Mid-sand toned facing brick with a finely-graded surface texture

Engineering brick made from a light-colored clay

This facing brick made from a pale clay has a subtle variation in surface color

This facing brick has a wave-textured surface and mottled color

Light sand-colored facing brick with a coarsely-graded surface texture

For a mellow, textured appearance use secondhand stocks

Mixing materials (left) *Knapped (split) flints set in mortar, and stone blocks have been used to create a checkerboard effect which, softened by patches of yellow lichen, is texturally interesting and makes a striking visual impact.*

Engineering brick displaying one of the many mottled effects available

Blue engineering brick has a hard, slick appearance that suits modern surroundings

For a warm-looking wall use terracotta-colored facing brick

Concrete blocks are available in larger unit sizes than brick

Low-grade engineering brick is cheaper and not as strong as the standard version

This concrete block is made from a finer-grade aggregate than the one above

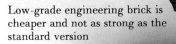

Sand-faced engineering brick has a "gritty" appearance

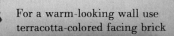

FENCING

Fencing is versatile and has many uses in the small-space garden. High panels of solid fencing can be used to create a wall-like barrier that will provide privacy and shelter, with the advantage that it is cheaper, easier to erect and lighter than walls (thus ideal for roof-spaces and balconies). Openwork fencing, or trellis, is often used to decorate or extend the height of existing walls.

Other types of fencing can be used as a boundary demarcation which, rather than acting as a barrier, will give you a glimpse of the outside world and increase the feeling of space in your small patch. Within a small garden-space different types of fencing can be used to screen unsightly structures, provide shelter (for both people and plants), create secluded areas, frame interesting glimpses or features, or as a decorative support for climbing or trailing plants.

There are dozens of different types of fencing; (a selection is shown in detail on pp.102–3). Some are ready-made, such as stockade fencing or trellis which are bought in panels. Others can be constructed, for instance practical board-on-board wood fencing, or bamboo lashed to rush matting. Depending on the height and shape of a fence and the material from which it is made the finished effect can be crisp and architectural or natural and rustic. Your choice will depend on what kind of barrier you need and the color and texture of the other materials used in your garden, such as brick, concrete, wood or metal.

Decorative divisions

It is often necessary to create some sort of division between a garden-space and its surroundings. You may need to divide your small front yard from the

Fenced garden
Horizontal larch pole fencing encloses this town garden, complementing the wooden steps and retaining walls within it. Tall boundary planting breaks up and visually softens the solid areas of fence, preventing them from overpowering the area within.

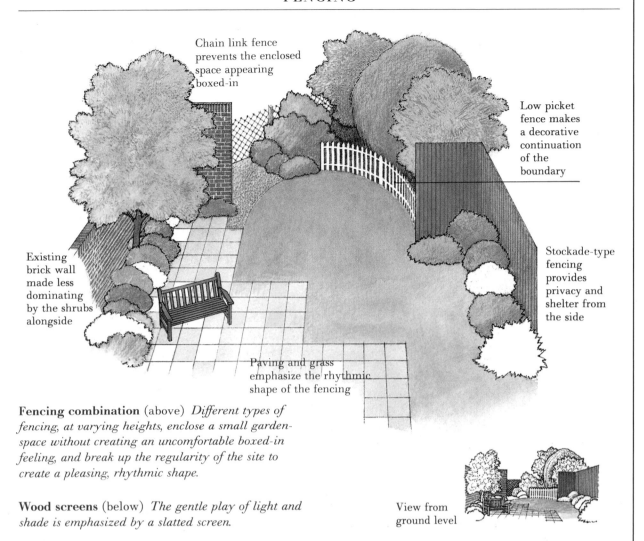

Chain link fence prevents the enclosed space appearing boxed-in

Low picket fence makes a decorative continuation of the boundary

Existing brick wall made less dominating by the shrubs alongside

Stockade-type fencing provides privacy and shelter from the side

Paving and grass emphasize the rhythmic shape of the fencing

Fencing combination (above) *Different types of fencing, at varying heights, enclose a small garden-space without creating an uncomfortable boxed-in feeling, and break up the regularity of the site to create a pleasing, rhythmic shape.*

Wood screens (below) *The gentle play of light and shade is emphasized by a slatted screen.*

View from ground level

street, or decide to replace a low chain and post fence that divides your strip of garden from its neighbors with something less minimal, which will give you at least some measure of privacy. Before choosing a particular type of fence ask yourself a few questions. Do you want to seclude your space from the outside world or do you just want some sort of attractive boundary demarcation? Or do you, for instance, wish to retain the pleasant view on one side of your garden and hide an ugly building on the other?

Fencing all round

In our zeal to give ourselves privacy and/or shelter we all too often box-in our space with high, solid fencing, which exaggerates the limitations of its size and can make it feel claustophobic too. There are several ways of minimizing this effect. One is to balance the area of fencing visually with a strong structural pattern within the garden, as you might if your space were surrounded by high walls. (See pp.92–3 for a three-dimensional build-up showing how to create a design that links the ground-pattern with the boundaries.) Another is to soften the outline of the fencing with bold masses of plant material. These two solutions have achieved the desired effect in the small garden

Decorative enclosure *This crisp cream picket fencing is entirely in character with the house it adjoins. In conjunction with a cream timber gate it makes a decorative boundary without overwhelming the small space it encloses.*

illustrated on page 98. Alternatively, different types and heights of fencing in combination with trees and large shrubs can be used to enclose your garden space without making it feel boxed-in, and give it a pleasing shape and pattern, like that shown at the top of page 99.

Openwork fencing

When dividing your small plot from that of your neighbors, consider the advantage of visually sharing space. Just a small panel of open fencing or lightly-planted trellis will counteract the boxed-in feeling, allowing for plenty of privacy in the remainder of the garden.

See-through fencing at any height will make a small space feel larger by allowing you to see beyond its boundaries. It will keep pets and children in as well as defining your boundaries. There are numerous types of open fencing (chain link and trellis to name but two); choose one that complements the style of your garden space.

Openwork fencing is a good support for climbing plants, which are ideal for small gardens because they take up so little ground space. They can be used to infill areas of see-through fencing to provide seasonal or year-round shelter and privacy, or grown up trelliswork to decorate a wall. Wires stretched between wooden verticals make an excellent form of fencing/plant support and can easily be constructed (see p.195).

Fencing is much lighter than walls and thus can be used to give a balcony or roof-space privacy and shelter, without imposing too much strain on the structure. Make sure that you are not infringing any planning regulations and the fence is well secured so the wind does not blow it over.

Fencing within the garden

Fencing (including railings or a metal fence) can be used within your garden space as well as around it. It can be used to hide parts of a garden you would rather not see – trash cans, an oil tank, or compost heap, for instance. Woven panel or close-board fencing will do the job admirably, as will open fencing covered with an evergreen climber.

A small area used for eating or sunbathing, will assume a room-like atmosphere if it is either partially or completely screened by fencing and, depending on your choice of fence, privacy and shelter from the wind. Screens made from fencing can be used purely for their visual effect too, to frame a feature within the garden, a piece of sculpture, for instance, or just to create interesting shapes in their own right. Another advantage is that a glimpse through a trellis or any other type of closely spaced screen will, by blurring the outlines of what lies beyond, give the smallest of spaces an illusion of size.

Trellised wall (right) *Trellis piers linked by thick rope decorate a brick wall.*

Color contrast (below and bottom) *Picket fencing can be painted to contrast with a simple backdrop, below, or simply offset by colorful planting, bottom.*

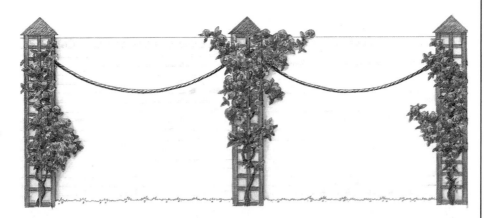

FENCING CHOICES

Fencing should suit its purpose as much as its location. Black trelliswork for instance, would make a sophisticated screen for an eating area, with minimal planting and chic, black furniture, whereas plain wooden picket fencing would make a simple, decorative boundary between a small, country-style town garden and the street.

Plastic, metal, and wood are the most common fencing materials (concrete is usually only used for fence posts). Many types of fencing are pre-fabricated and are assembled on site (see p.195 for details of fence post construction). Some such panels may be too large for your site. By designing your own fencing you can tailor it to fit the exact dimensions of your space, and to suit the style of the rest of your garden space.

Plastic suits urban locations better than rural ones and is maintenance free. Most prefabricated, plastic fencing is low-level and serves to define a boundary rather than enclose it. Metal fencing in the form of rolls of wire mesh and chain link (sometimes covered in plastic) is ideal for curving around awkwardly-shaped spaces. It can be supported by metal, concrete, or wood verticals, or fixed into a frame (see below).

There is a style of wooden fencing to suit just about every practical purpose and every location. Unless you use very expensive hardwoods, wood must be stripped of bark and then treated with a wood preservative, or sealed and then painted, to prevent decay. Wood rots if left in direct contact with the ground, so wooden posts should be placed in a metal shoe which in turn should be set in a concrete foundation, and wooden fencing panels raised slightly above the ground (see construction details on pp.195–6).

Plastic-coated chain link fencing in a wood frame

Panel fencing comprises horizontal slats

Bamboo lengths can be bound to make a solid or openwork screen

Wooden trellis can be used to decorate or extend the height of existing walls

Black iron chain, suitable for post and chain fencing

Painted picket fencing makes a decorative boundary

Closeboard fencing is built by nailing feather-edged verticals to horizontal rails

ENTRANCES AND EXITS

Entrances are important not just because "first impressions count" but because the only outside space that many town- and city-dwellers have is the small area between street and door – an alleyway, a path, or maybe just a doorstep.

New-style and old-style
The traditional approach to a house consists of three parts: a gate, a path (usually through a small garden) and a front door. These are usually designed together to give a stylistically unified look; the details of the gate matching those of the door, which in turn echo architectural characteristics of the house. But current urban living, with its high-rise apartments, conversions, split-levels, and the need for security makes for unconventional and less obvious approaches – round the sides of buildings, through passageways, down

Entrance patio *For sheer style this Mediterranean entrance would be hard to improve. The paving acts as a neutral canvas for the brilliant colors of the paintwork, fabric and planting.*

steps, or through security gates. These can nevertheless be styled so they make a satisfying transition between the street and the home. Whether the approach to your home is traditional or unconventional you can emphasize it, brighten it, and make it welcoming too.

Setting the mood
The material of your path, passageway, or entrance area, the style of your gate, the color of your door, its fixtures and fittings and the tubs and pots around it should all suit the style of your home and set the mood for what lies within it.

Traditional gate (right) *A typical Continental gate which is decorative and provides security – the owner can see who is there before opening up, yet the passer-by has a pleasant glimpse through.*

Bold entrance (far right) *A contemporary counterpart of the traditional gate on the left. Its bold design leaves visitors in no doubt that they have arrived.*

Linking the style of home and entrance *This gray, wooden gate blends in with the muted style of the structures around it and matches the shutters and door surround behind it. These visual links combine to make an entrance that suits the character of the area it encloses as well as the house it leads to.*

Let your choice be guided by the architectural style of your home. Try to echo its characteristics, in the shape, color, materials, or decorative patterning of your door or gate. There are as many types of gates as there are architectural styles, ranging from ornate late nineteenth-century metal gates, to cottage picket gates and ranch-style gates. (See p.196 for the construction details of different types of gate.) Echoing the style of a front door in particular (its shape, color, material), in that of a gate will visually link the two and unify the space between them. Look too at the structure your door or gate pierces. A slick brick wall, for instance, would be best suited to a crisp, modern design in smooth painted wood, or metal, whereas a textured stone wall would be complemented by a more rusticated design in natural wood (see the illustrations of different styles of entrance on p.106). A front door or gate should also suit the character of the rest of the street, for they are very much part of the community.

Gates for privacy and security

Many people who live in urban areas are becoming increasingly security-conscious and so have front gates designed for security, which are high, robust, and are almost always controlled from indoors. This type of gate is usually made from metal rather than wood and when well-designed and in keeping with the surroundings, like those shown above, can be attractive and functional.

Privacy too, is often sought by those who live on busy streets. In conjunction with a high wall or closeboard fencing, a solid or louvered gate (made from wood or metal) can be used to enclose the area between street and home, giving complete privacy from passers-by (see p.196 for construction details of a sheet metal gate). Small areas enclosed like this, and paved or surfaced with gravel perhaps, and furnished with a few plants in pots, and seating, can assume a pleasant courtyard quality, making the entrance to the home a congenial and private space for sitting outside and in which children can play in safety.

Though other types of gate (low wooden gates, iron railing gates, and slatted gates) can prevent small children and pets from getting out they are primarily a decorative break in a boundary, rather than a barrier against intrusion, both physical and visual. They mark an entrance and give both the passer-by and person within a glimpse of what lies beyond. Low gates, by making a break in a solid boundary wall for instance, have the advantage of making a confined space seem larger and preventing it from appearing boxed-in.

The approach
Though the approach to your home, be it a regular-shaped space with a path, some winding steps or a narrow passageway, should be safe and practical you should aim also to make it a stylish extension of your home. If such an area is your only outside space you will undoubtedly wish to make the most of it. Design ideas for narrow passageways are shown on pages 76–7 and for steps on pages 78–9.

Gate and door styles
1 *This traditional wooden door blends in with an old stone wall and gives the small courtyard entrance within complete privacy.*
2 *A painted wooden door, surrounded by classical pilasters and an architrave, sets the mood for the style of the small garden it encloses.*
3 *The shape of the terracotta finials above this modern iron gate are echoed by its round motif which draws the eye to the door beyond.*

A narrow path leading straight through a small area between the street and a front door will, by dividing it up, make it appear smaller. Rather than build a narrow path, pave a small entrance area in an overall pattern (see p.115 for the visual effect of different paving patterns) or lay it with gravel, for this will give it a homogenous look and make it appear larger.

Where the paving's primary purpose is to provide a service pathway, however, ensure slippery surfaces, planting, and changes of level are kept to a minimum. Materials with textured surfaces, such as brick give a better foothold than smooth ones like concrete.

Often, the area directly between the street and home has to be used for parking, and is in effect a driveway. Make sure that access for cars is free of obstacles or narrow gates that make driving in and out a test of nerves. The ground surface should have drainage in the form of gulleys leading to a dry well or soakaway, or a fall into the surrounding ground, so that water used for washing your car will drain away.

Doors and doorsteps
Doors, whether they are on the street or set back from it, can be decorated so they are welcoming and set the mood for what lies behind them. Make the most of painted color either on the door itself or to pick out moldings or other architectural features on its surround.

The size of a doorstep can be increased by building a small plinth either side of it, or by extending it forwards. A well-placed pot or piece of sculpture on the doorstep, or a decorative garland hanging from the door will make an entrance both obvious and welcoming to visitors. If your door is on the street make sure that any decorative

1 *Traditional wooden door*   2 *Classical style entrance*   3 *Modern iron gate*

items are firmly attached, for weight alone is no deterrent to the determined filcher. A pergola-type structure attached at one end to the wall around a door and supported at the other by freestanding verticals is a good way of leading visitors to less obviously situated entrances. (Pergolas are shown on the following pages.)

Often trash cans have to be kept near a front door. If there is room, the cans can be hidden in a built-in cupboard (made from brick, wood or whatever material most suits the style of your house), perhaps with a plant container that is integral to the design (see the Special Design Case on p.86). Alternatively, they can be hidden behind an evergreen shrub, or a trelliswork screen covered with an evergreen climber; English Ivy, *Hedera helix* 'Goldheart', for example, would do the trick most effectively.

Entering with style *This striking architectural treatment of a basement entrance makes a dramatic contrast with the classical portico behind.*

It becomes obvious when seeking someone's home, particularly from behind a driving wheel at night, how badly many people mark them, if at all. Illuminating your front door and the number or name of your home will make it easier for visitors to find you and safer if you are returning home late at night. Site the source of light so its beam shines upwards to create a warm, subtle glow, rather than a harsh, dark shadow created by a light shining downwards from a high position (different lighting effects are shown on p.136). Choose a light fitting that suits the style of your place – an "olde-worlde" carriage lamp can be all that is needed to ruin the effect of a slick, modern entrance.

PERGOLAS

Perhaps the image of the pergola that springs most readily to mind is that of a vine-entwined structure like that shown below, used in sunny Mediterranean climates to create shade and form a covered transition between buildings. Pergolas have many other practical and visual uses in a small space – they can form a semi-covered room, or a plant-covered arbor, or be used to strengthen some aspect of a garden's design.

Directional pergolas

Pergolas, like the one shown below, left, and on the opposite page, which lead from one space to another, are what I call dynamic or directional pergolas. In contrast, those that cover a wider area, and define a space rather than lead through it, are static in nature.

Directional pergolas can be free-standing or connected to a building. The free-standing type draws the eye down its length thereby shortening the foreground perspective. There are situations where this is desirable, for instance where a pergola leads the eye to, and frames a view, or an entrance, or like that on the opposite page, where it is constructed over a path. However, the ground on either side of directional pergolas tends to become merely the "left-overs" in small spaces.

Directional pergolas attached to the side of a building create a colonnade effect and are useful for covering an entrance or keeping the sun from rooms inside. If, in a hot climate, the pergola's structure and planting alone do not provide enough shade, a roller blind can be attached to the top of the pergola and pulled across to block out

Sheltered space (above and right) *The pergola, above, shelters a front door on a hot Mediterranean street, and that on the right a deck in the United States, creating a room-like setting for summer-living outside.*

Directional pergola (opposite page) *This wooden pergola constructed over a tiled path has a forceful, dynamic effect.*

the sun. Or consider split and rattan cane blinds to fill in the gaps between the horizontals. As well as providing extra shade these will create interesting shadows on the ground as the sun moves overhead. In colder climes, however, blinds are not usually necessary as the spreading, summertime foliage of annual climbers is probably enough to soften the sun's effect, while in winter, the stark pergola frame allows the light in.

Static pergolas

Static pergolas, those that do not lead in one direction, but cover a larger area, a terrace, for instance, or even the entire garden, are a good way of extending the mood of an interior, and creating visually, at least, an additional room outside. By providing a ceiling (in the form of the pergola's horizontals) it is possible to create the feeling of being in a room outside, thus weakening the barriers between inside and outside and increasing the overall feeling of space.

Such static pergolas are rarely free-standing structures, with uprights at both ends of the horizontals. In a small space there is certainly not enough room for this. Rather, the horizontals are connected to a wall at one end, and sail outwards to

Defining and enclosing space (above and below)
A simple metal-hooped pergola, above, entwined with climbing roses, emphasizes the shape of a path, while the solid vine-covered wooden and stone pergola, below, encloses a small corner site.

meet the verticals which rise from the edge of the total covered space. Or uprights may not be required at all, the horizontals simply bridging the gap between two walls, for instance two boundary walls, or a house wall and a boundary wall.

Pergolas on roofs

Roof gardens are often rather exposed, not only to the wind and the great expanse of sky above, but to surrounding buildings, and as a consequence they are not always very congenial. A pergola constructed on a roof will give the space a sheltered feel and, if covered with tough climbing plants will protect against sun and wind.

It is important to check the strength of a roof before constructing a pergola, for its weight can be quite considerable (you may need planning permission too). Metal frames are lighter than wood and if there are walls either side of the roof area metal wires or rope can be used.

Planting

Pergolas, whether free-standing or adjoining a building, make a wonderful host to climbing plants – one of the most attractive aspects of a plant-covered pergola is the quality of dappled light that filters through the foliage. Plant material will soften the overall effect of the structure and help provide shade and privacy, the latter being of great benefit in towns and cities where gardens are so often overlooked. Growing plants vertically is also an excellent way of saving space at ground level.

Architectural extension *This painted wooden pergola, covered with wisteria, makes a perfect extension to the clapboarded house it adjoins.*

Remember, however, to consider the weight of any envisaged planting in relation to the strength of the pergola, particularly if you wish to train plants along wires or rope. Bear in mind too the density of the plant's foliage and the length of time it is in leaf, for this will affect the amount of shade provided. Evergreen climbers, for instance, may create too much shade in the winter months when maximum light is needed.

Pergolas for proportion

In many urban areas where garden spaces are not in scale with surrounding buildings a pergola's horizontals can be used to lower the height of the space and create an aesthetically pleasing and proportioned area that is comfortable to be in. If the style of the pergola suits the architecture around it, it will link the space covered more closely with its surroundings. One of the most useful facets of any sort of pergola is that its horizontals, or shadows cast by them, can provide a useful visual framework within which to work when designing the rest of the garden. The shapes created by the horizontals can be echoed in similarly proportioned areas of paving, gravel and planting. This will help create the integrated, "all of a piece" look so visually satisfactory in a small space garden.

PERGOLA CHOICE

It is important that the pergola as a whole should be in keeping with the mood and style of the buildings around it. As shown in the photographs on these pages, materials can be treated in different ways to create very individual looks.

A pergola's horizontals can be made in varying dimensions and from a wide range of materials, depending on how much light you wish to have from above and the look you want. The verticals must be made from a material strong enough to support the weight of the horizontals. Visually speaking, horizontals should be considerably heavier than uprights. The drawings on page 197 show different styles of pergola construction.

Wood is the most common material for pergolas. Softwood can be used planed or sawn, depending on whether you want a smooth or textured surface. Hardwood is much more expensive, but it is more durable. Any type of wood can be painted, stained, or just treated with a wood preservative. The ends of the pergola horizontals, like those shown opposite, can be shaped to echo architectural features.

Metal is also suitable for constructing pergolas. It is lighter than pieces of lumber and does not create such an impression of division. To create a pergola that is lighter still, use tensioned wire or brightly-colored weatherproof rope as the horizontals, and suspend them between two walls.

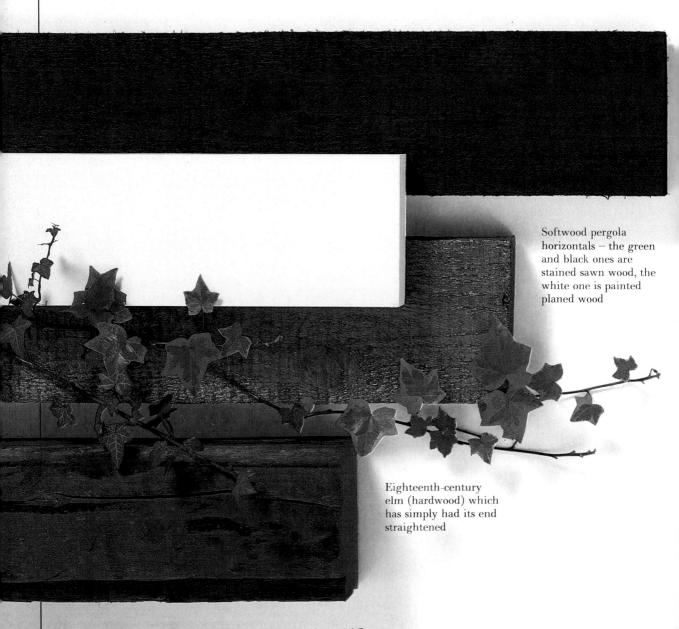

Softwood pergola horizontals – the green and black ones are stained sawn wood, the white one is painted planed wood

Eighteenth-century elm (hardwood) which has simply had its end straightened

Sawn softwood pergola horizontal stained darker than its natural color by a wood preservative

Wire stretched by a tensioner to form a taut pergola horizontal

Painted softwood horizontal cut to a decorative shape, with painted scaffolding pole upright

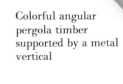

Colorful angular pergola timber supported by a metal vertical

PAVING

The surface material you have outside should suit your garden as much as the flooring you have inside your home suits its various rooms and, just like choosing an interior flooring, you should consider the style, cost and practical suitability of different materials.

Paving, in all its various forms, is one of the most useful of surfaces outside. It provides hard-standing for furniture, pots, and other features, requires little maintenance and can act either as a neutral backdrop or as a feature in its own right.

Paving designs
Your first consideration, whatever your final choice of paving material, should be to decide on a paving design, by which I mean the overall combination of shapes as well as the position of any individual paving units within these. It is important to decide on this early on, for different paving designs can radically alter the look of a space. The drawings on the opposite page show the effect of different paving patterns.

Broadly speaking, paving patterns can be divided into those that are static and those that are dynamic. Static paving patterns hold the eye

within the site, or one part of it, whilst dynamic paving patterns lead the eye through it.

Some paving patterns have the effect of visually dividing up a space into individual mini-rooms; others, usually those which are very densely-patterned, hold the eye in one spot. A very bland pattern, or none at all, will emphasize the overall shape of the area paved and act as a neutral backdrop to other aspects of the garden's design.

Dynamic paving patterns
In contrast, dynamic paving patterns create a sense of movement and visual pull. In a conventional, comparatively large garden space, there might be traditional pathways of hard surfacing through lawn and planting. These strong lines always lead the eye and are dynamic. In the small garden where an area of paving might cover the entire space available, you can only create a dynamic scheme through the arrangement of a pattern within the paving or by aligning areas that flow one to another so they lead the eye.

Linear paving patterns will work where the visual pull has a satisfying conclusion, for instance a pleasing view, a sculptural feature, or, like a path

leading to a front door, has a practical function. A static surfacing design is usually preferable when paving an enclosed space with no one point of focus, such as a terrace used for meals outside.

Whether you choose a static or dynamic paving design, you will increase the apparent dimensions of a small space by having a simple paving pattern and scaling-up the other features. Conversely, a heavily-patterned arrangement will create a "busy" effect and emphasize its smallness.

Types of paving

The type of paving material you choose will depend on the mood and style of the enclosure, and the materials that are available locally.

Take into account the texture as well as the color of different paving materials before making your choice. The mood of a brick house, for example, with some brick walling and timber fencing in the garden, would probably be best sustained by brick paving or wooden decking. Stone paving, in this instance, would be less suitable, for it would probably fight with the brick and the use of a third material would make the overall design too busy. Conversely, a space adjacent to a stone building, with stone boundary walls, probably calls for the use of wood and more stone (or concrete slabs of a similar aggregate) as the ground surface, for brick or tiles would be visually too weak.

PAVING DESIGNS

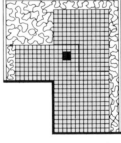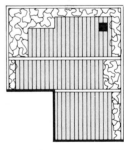

1 This paving pattern gives a diagonal pull towards the top right-hand corner.

2 Paved steps running right across the space give this layout a strong pull towards the feature.

These layouts show how broad paving patterns and the arrangement of the units within them can create very different effects in a small space. The bottom left-hand corner represents a house; the black square a feature.

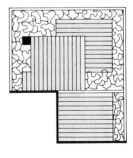

3 The paving pattern here creates a sense of movement.

Creative combination (left) *Paving is a versatile and practical alternative to small areas of grass – here large gray concrete units push forwards to meet diagonally-laid, honey-colored bricks in a vigorous design. Planting in tubs and through the paving softens the effect.*

Colored paving (top) *Randomly-shaped concrete paving slabs have been colored and arranged to create a lively mosaic.*

Patterned pathway (above) *Bricks between concrete paving units make a strong geometrical pattern.*

PAVING CHOICE

Natural, local paving materials are usually the most practical and suited to the environment. In rural areas this is likely to be local stone. However, in urban areas, where there is unlikely to be a common natural building material, concrete and brick are the most universal building media.

There are numerous forms of precast concrete paving, ranging from those resembling clay pavers, through slabs of varying shapes and thicknesses to pieces the size of railway ties. Generally, the plainer and more subdued the better – a single virulent, heavily-textured paver can look dramatic, but in a mass will be disastrous. Concrete can be laid *in situ*, and then brushed to expose its aggregate before it sets (see p.198).

As well as brick pavers, especially manufactured for paving, patio blocks, and facing bricks can be used, though the latter are softer than the former and liable to crumble. These, and other small units, such as granite blocks, and cobbles, are ideal for paving small and even awkwardly-shaped areas. Paving construction is shown on page 198.

Consider all the surfacing materials at your disposal as a palette from which you can choose to contrast and complement the various structures of your garden. Paving an area in the same material as the surrounding walls is a good way of giving a small space a unified look and binding together the various elements of its design.

Bear in mind practical considerations too. Some materials, such as certain smooth, precast pavers become slippery in rain and snow; others, like brick, give a good foothold.

Proprietary concrete paving blocks

Smooth round concrete slab

Patio or paving blocks manufactured in many local clay colors – they create a clean crisp effect

Two sizes of rough-edged granite blocks

Hexagonal concrete paving slab

Plain concrete edging

Mixed pavings *Slabs of concrete with a brushed aggregate finish and cobbles in coarse gravel* *have been arranged in precast concrete to create a satisfying design of varying texture and color.*

Fluted neoclassical style edging

Wire-cut clay blocks

A glazed barley-sugar edging

Textured blue stock brick

Concrete coping

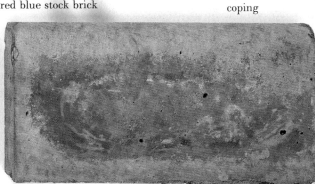

SOFT SURFACING

Gravel and other "soft" surfacing materials, such as pebbles, shingle and bark, are practical, versatile, and visually pleasing. They are cheaper and easier to lay than hard surfacing materials such as concrete and stone, and make an ideal textural transition, being softer than paving and harder than grass or ground cover planting.

Gravel and pebbles can be laid loose and this is the ideal way of surfacing tight spaces that are too awkward to pave. There is one drawback, however, and this is that they are rather difficult and somewhat noisy to walk on, but this can act as a deterrent to burglars.

Loose gravel and pebbles are also ideal for laying in places where little will grow and paving would be impractical, for instance through and under trees. Leaves can be raked or blown off to leave them looking neat.

Gravel that has been rolled into a consolidated layer of binding gravel (this is unwashed and retains a clay constituent) forms a semi-hard surface. This construction detail is shown on page 198. Treated in this way it is a perfect surface to have alongside a paved terrace area on to which people can overflow at parties, and being porous it can absorb an overflow of water too.

In small urban spaces a very crisp, neat look can be obtained by using shingle or gravel instead of small areas of grass, which require considerably more maintenance, do not wear as well, and often

Hard and soft surfaces (above) *A pale gravel creates a sharp, clean effect in combination with dark-colored railway ties and the deep-brown spiky leaves of New Zealand sedge* (Uncinia unciniata).

Gravel garden (right) *This gravel has been rolled to form a semi-hard surface, perfect for taking the wear and tear of chair legs. Its pale color and crunchy texture make it an excellent foil to the smooth dark-green leaves of palms* (Trachycarpus fortunei) *and bamboos* (Arundinaria murielae).

GRAVEL PATTERNS

Gravel garden *Sandy gravel has been raked around an island of stone in this Japanese-style garden designed by Patrick Watson.*

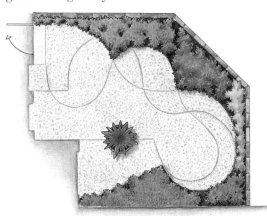

Abstract shapes *A swirling design for a small walled area using different colored loose gravels divided by ribbons of aluminum.*

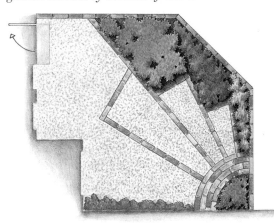

Radial design *Two colors of gravel radiate outwards from an area of corner planting. The brick used to divide the gravel is an integral part of the design.*

look tired throughout the winter. Gravel that is to be used in this way should be contained by brick edging or some other hard surface.

Planting in soft surfaces

Shrubs, lower herbs, seasonal bulbs and perennials grow happily through gravel, shingle and smallish pebbles in a layer no more than 100mm (4 in) deep. The binding layer acts as a mulch and is an ideal medium in which seeds can germinate. After all, scree gardens are composed mainly of gravel in well-drained layers – the natural medium for growing alpine plants.

Planting in areas of gravel instead of bare earth confined to beds will help create a random, relaxed look, by visually binding planted areas more naturally with those of a paved area or neighboring pathway. This will also increase the apparent size of a small space, for the fewer ground divisions there are, the less cramped it will appear.

Textural combinations

Japanese gardeners have used gravel as a ground surfacing for centuries, raking it into abstract patterns that simulate maritime eddies and currents swirling around islands of rock and moss.

As the photograph at the top of this page shows, this is a technique that can be copied in small spaces to great effect. However, it does call for regular, if not daily care, because every shower of rain and every footprint erodes the pattern.

Just as effective, and considerably less time-consuming, is the combination of unraked gravel or pebbles with boulders and rocks. This is a good way of giving a small garden an interesting abstract look. Quarried rocks are usually angular, but rounded boulders are sometimes produced during the grading process of washed shingle.

Gravel designs

The seventeenth-century French and Italians also used gravel between the areas of box hedging in their formally-patterned *parterres*. Gravel can be put to the same formal use in small spaces too, and can be used in conjunction with well-defined areas of planting to create a geometrical pattern.

Different colors and sizes of gravel can be used to create patterns, varying from a formal checkerboard effect to looser, more abstract shapes. The two drawings on the left show contrasting gravel designs suitable for a small-space garden. Brick or thin strips of wood or aluminum should be used to divide up the gravel; the former can be treated as part of the design.

As well as being an effective way of decorating ground-level spaces, patterned gravel is a useful medium for covering a roof which is looked down on, or bringing interest to a dark well in which plants are unable to flourish.

SOFT SURFACING CHOICE

Many different looks can be created depending on the color and gauge of gravel or pebble chosen. Gravel consists of natural rock chippings, so potentially there are as many different sorts of gravel as there are types of rock. The choice ranges from white and creamy beige, to gray, red, brown and black. The range of colors of river-washed shingle or dredged pea shingle, both rounded by the action of water, is not quite as extensive.

Both gravel and shingle suit just about all locations, but bear in mind that they tend to be swept up when snow is being cleared and a pale gravel can produce rather a lot of glare in open areas exposed to harsh sunlight. Shingle and pea shingle are more suitable for children to play on because, unlike gravel, they have no sharp edges.

The least expensive type of soft surfacing will probably be that produced from rock native to your area. In mountainous areas this is likely to be quarried chippings; in areas near the sea or a large river, pea shingle. In urban areas gravel will have been imported from rural areas, so costs vary.

Gravel, shingle, pebbles and bark can be used in conjunction with hard materials. Panels of gravel within an area paved in brick or concrete will soften the overall effect and introduce a satisfying textural contrast.

When laid next to a uniformly hard surface such as concrete paving, gravel does not need an edging. However, if it is laid next to grass or a planted area it will need to be contained if you do not intend the two to merge. Wood, brick, or concrete can be used for edging (see p.117) as can metal or plastic. Choose whichever edging most suits the overall look of your garden or some of its detailing. A drawing on page 198 illustrates how to set an edging in poured concrete alongside an area of gravel or shingle.

Gray granite chippings can be laid loose as an alternative to fine-textured gravel

White limestone chippings (coarse grade) can be laid loose for a clean crisp look

Washed pea shingle has rounded edges and is safer for children to play on than sharp-edged gravel

White granite chippings like these can be used to create patterns

Textural arrangement *Gravel and large pebbles create a satisfying arrangement of textures, rather like that of a dried-up stream bed.*

Fine-textured washed shingle is a good alternative to soil for planting

Bark can be laid through trees and shrubs to create a soft organic look

Honey-colored rock chippings can create a "warm" look when used alongside soft-colored brick

Fine horticultural grit can be used on its own or mixed with gravel as a medium for planting

DECKS

Decking, which has been common in the United States and on the Continent for years, is a comparatively new introduction in the United Kingdom, even though the step between it and a wooden balcony is a small one. In fact, decking can be used to create a balcony garden where there was no usable space before. But it is not necessarily tied to a building, for it can be used as a surfacing material at ground level.

The uses of decking

The deck really comes into its own when used in conjunction with a property on a hillside, where, raised on posts, it can be used to create a level platform on the side of the building facing away from the slope. The deck makes the transition out from the elevated first floor, and steps from the deck lead to ground level. This type of decking is often the only feasible way of creating a level space outside the house.

Traditionally in the United States, older houses were built so the living area is above ground level, leaving space beneath for a cellar and, similarly, many split-level houses built today have their main living areas above ground level. In both cases the deck is a way of extending the upper level to create a usable outside room.

In the United States and on the Continent low-level decks are often built instead of brick or stone terraces. This is because wood is much cheaper than in the United Kingdom and suits the character of the houses, which often have wooden clapboarding or shingled roofs. Low-level decking can give a small space a pleasing unified look when

Low-level decking (above) *Decking can be used as an alternative to paving at ground level. The combination of the wooden door, fencing, furniture and decking creates a simple unified look that stylishly enhances the narrow passageway.*

Treetop decking (right) *This raised deck has been cut to encompass existing trees and create a treetop retreat. Moisture in the form of rain or snow can reach the trees' roots through the gaps between the wooden horizontals.*

used in conjunction with wooden fencing, as in the passageway, far left. It need not be used to cover the whole of an area. Interesting patterns and satisfying textural contrasts can be created by combining small areas of deck with stone or concrete paving. Decking is also a pleasing surface to have alongside water, around a swimming pool or a small water feature.

Wooden decking also makes an ideal surfacing for city roof gardens. Square wooden panels, in similar dimensions to paving slabs can be clamped together to provide a sympathetic flooring that is not as heavy as concrete or brick. The panels should be laid on a wooden base above the roof finish, so that water can drain to an outlet.

Ideally decks should be made of a hardwood which needs no preservative treatment. Softwood, which is not as hardy, must not only be planed to prevent splintering but needs preservative treatment and becomes slippery to walk on in wet weather. The weather makes decking less popular in a damp climate as it rarely dries out. On the Continent and in the United States, where temperatures are more extreme, a deck which might be covered in a thick layer of snow in winter does at least have a chance to dry out in the summer months. Also in the United States there is pressurized (weather-resistant) lumber.

Construction

Low-level decking is not hard to construct. The decking timbers rest on a slatted structure of beams and joists supported by posts held in concrete piers. The construction of a simple low-level deck is illustrated on page 199. A more ambitious use of decking on a hillside or as an extension above ground level requires the expertise of an architect.

Raised garden space *The crisp lines of this wooden deck continue the feel of the house it adjoins and make a congenial extension to the inside living area.*

STEPS

Not only are many small gardens in locations where they can only be reached by steps, but for some a flight of steps *is* the garden. As well as enabling you to get from A to B, steps can be decorated so they are a stylish addition to your garden, or a mini-garden in their own right.

Decorating and building steps

Pots and containers are a simple and effective way of decorating steps and, if planted, of integrating the soft forms of flowers and foliage with the hard ones of structure. Painting steps or adjacent walls in a color that tones in well with surrounding structures will give dowdy steps a new lease of life. A handrail (see p.200) can be a stylish and practical addition to service steps, particularly those which are steep. Good lighting will make steps a pleasure to look at, and safer at night.

As well as constructing new access steps or replacing old ones you may wish to build a shallow run of steps, as opposed to broader stepped changes of level (see p.200), within your garden to give it a sense of movement and sculptural interest that will make it appear larger than it really is. (See p.200 for construction details of a flight of steps.)

Very different effects can be created according to the overall shape of the steps and the angle they lie at in relation to surrounding structures. The three designs below left, are suitable for service steps (leading up to a front door, for instance) and steps within a small garden space.

Step dimensions and materials

The ideal dimensions for a set of service steps are a maximum height of 20cm (8 in) and a tread width of 50cm (20 in); these will give a gentle pace. Steps that take a curved or zig-zag route may need wider treads, encouraging an even more leisurely pace.

Steps built in the same or a similar material as surrounding structures will blend in well and become a pleasing part of the structural pattern of a garden or building. However, safety must be considered when building service steps. Stone and wood, for instance, become very slippery after rain and frost, whereas textured materials like old stock brick, or a smooth material, like concrete,

Feature steps (right) *These simple stone steps are softened by an informal planting of coneflower (Rudbeckia cv.) and various decorative grasses.*

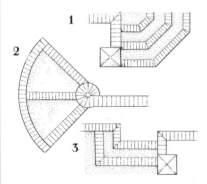

Steps designs (above) *The steps in these plans are just as suitable for entrance steps as linking changes of level in a small space. Each set lies at a different angle giving them sculptural interest.*
1 Steps that turn at 45° give a sense of lateral movement.
2 Wide steps on a curve allow a leisurely pace.
3 A 90° return give steps a spacious feel.

Stepped gardens (above and right) *Terracotta pots of succulents emphasize the turn in the wooden entrance steps, above, while geraniums, right, accentuate the gentle rhythm of a stepped wall.*

infilled with a rougher material, such as stone, will give a better foothold. Do not introduce plant material into the pattern of service steps, for this will make them unsafe at night and in the wet.

"Inherited" steps

When spacious old houses or apartment blocks are converted into smaller units, steps designed originally for use as a back staircase, or a fire escape, sometimes become used as the main entrance. Conversely, grand old steps sometimes become the route to a small apartment.

An ugly old metal staircase can be given a new lease of life with a lick of fresh paint or partially concealed with a climber. The width of grand steps can be reduced by removing some of the horizontal tread on either side, and introducing plant material in its place.

When large gardens are divided up, steps that once led from one area to another are sometimes inherited by the owner of a smaller patch, for whom they serve no practical purpose. Instead of removing such steps integrate them into your overall design by treating them as a sculptural feature, which could be a focal point for the pattern of your planting, or informal seating.

WATER

Water has a compelling quality and can bring light and life to the most limited of spaces. It is both versatile and predictable (the latter being something that plants are not), and lends itself to being contained within an architectural setting.

An area of water, however styled, should be treated as an integral part of the garden's pattern, and its dimensions should be considered in relation to the height of surrounding boundaries.

Creative uses of water

Obviously lack of space will inhibit the quantity of water that can be included in a small garden. However, water can easily be incorporated into some sort of feature, and if ground space is very limited it need not necessarily be one that is horizontal, for what immediately springs to my mind is the use of falling water. The effects you can achieve range from the merest trickle from a wall spout, to a vertical wall of water.

Though water can be cold and depressing, if used properly it will always be eye-catching or even mesmerizing. A very significant factor that few consider is that the running, splashing, or trickling of flowing water, as well as being visually pleasing can help to block out urban noise. On a hot day the sight and sound of gently running water will have a cooling effect too.

An area of still water at ground level in a garden creates a mirrored setting for surrounding features. A dark internal lining at the bottom of a pool of water will intensify reflections further whereas a light-colored glazed tile finish will reduce them. The latter treatment will tempt you to look into the water's depths, rather than its surface, adding yet another dimension to your garden space. Sunlight playing on the surface of still water produces a Hockney-like, cellular pattern, and if near a building a reflection rather like light dancing on a ceiling.

Flat planes of water can also act as a foil to planting, either in the water or adjacent to it, reeds and water lilies for instance, or overhanging blossoms. This is a way of linking part of your garden's ground-pattern to three-dimensional plant forms. (See pp.190–2 for plants suitable for growing in and around water.) If plants are used in association with moving water, a fountain or water splash for instance, the relationship between structure and planting becomes more vibrant.

Watery retreat (left) *A small pool is the center of attraction in a tiny fenced Continental garden.*

A mirrored setting (above and right) *Bold luxuriant planting above, both in and around the water, softens the hard lines of the L-shaped pool, right, that defines the shape of a town-house terrace in Washington D.C.*

Design principles *These drawings show how to build up a watery picture with a small pool in an enclosed space.*

A formally-shaped sunken pool that is in scale with the surrounding walls

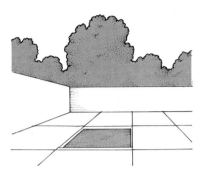

By raising the pool the relationship with the surrounding walls is strengthened

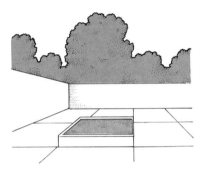

The water takes on a sculptural form when two pools are interconnected

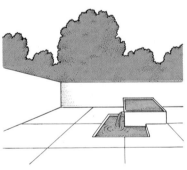

Alternatively, plant forms can be used to make a link with the boundary walls

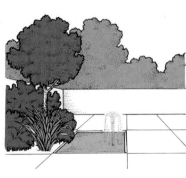

The most exciting composition – interconnecting pools are counterpoised with the planted mass

Water as sculptural decoration *Shallow water-filled containers can be moved around to make various sculptural arrangements – a simple way of introducing water to a small-space garden, bringing the light of twinkling reflections and attracting birds.*

Planes of water can be contained at different heights to create a visual relationship between the ground plan and the boundary. The focus of interest can be water flowing from one plane to another, or the "New York plaza" effect can be created, obviously on a small scale, by allowing it to form a waterfall down a wall.

Water can also be used as sculptural decoration within a basic layout, rather than as an integral part of the garden's structure. Because water has such a compelling quality, it is important that a water feature intended as decoration is contained within a strong garden plan to prevent it dominating the scene.

Water can be used as sculptural decoration in the form of a wall splash, or an arrangement of water-filled containers, either free-standing, like those above, or interconnected.

Decorative pools
Natural-looking pools of water usually look out of character in tight urban spaces. However, though I have a personal dislike for the Japanese water garden out of its natural habitat, its more mannered approach to wildness is more sympathetic to urban locations, than the soft-edged garden pond which only suits truly rural settings.

In the main, unless extremely well-designed and crafted, the simpler the use of water in a small space the more effective it will be. A tiny courtyard in the south of France comes to mind, in which there is a shallow pool, with a pattern of fish modelled in the tiles that line it – so simple, but constantly compelling. The water must be sparkling clean for this sort of effect and this means excellent maintenance. There are many water-cleaning devices on the market, of varying sophistication – their installation requires specialist advice. (See small pool construction on p.201.)

Water to relax and exercise in

"Lap" pools are becoming more and more popular with the health-conscious. They are pieces of water designed for swimming laps in, and need not be more than 3m (10 ft) in width, but should be no shorter than 7m (23 ft) in length. It is just about possible to incorporate a lap pool of the minimum dimensions in a small garden, though little space will be left for anything else.

Any type of swimming pool should work within a scaled layout. Often the relationship between pool shape and size and the rest of the garden is ill-considered. Pear-shaped or kidney-shaped pools, so beloved by their manufacturers, are often fitted into an angular space, with the result that the areas left around them look awkward both in relation to the pool itself and to the remainder of the garden site.

A plunge pool (a pool large enough to immerse the body in) is a much smaller alternative. If fitted with a wave machine it can provide a force of water against which to swim and exercise and also make a natural focal point for social occasions in the summer months.

Even smaller in scale are the jacuzzi and the hot tub (or even a combination of the two), which can be included in a sheltered space. If they are close to the house they can be used in the winter. Immersing yourself in warm water with only the head in sub-zero temperatures can be a stimulating, not to say bizarre, experience.

It is essential when having warm water outside to have some sort of cover to conserve the heat so expensively generated. Bear in mind that the simpler the shape of the pool the easier it will be to cover. Automatic quilts are available, which at the press of a button glide from under the coping of the pool across the surface of the water. Covering the pool will also keep it cleaner.

Indoor-outdoor swimming pool *A sliding, glazed section enables this pool to be used inside during the winter and outside during the summer – a neat way of including a swimming pool in a limited space.*

POTS AND CONTAINERS

Pots and containers are an invaluable ingredient for furnishing and adding to the style of your outside space. I do not use the word garden here deliberately, for it does not accurately describe many of the locations where pots are particularly useful. They are one of the most practical ways of decorating roofs, decks, balconies and windows as well as the more usual ground level areas.

What can a pot do?

Pots not only make a strong statement of style, through their shape, color and decoration, but when carefully positioned they also help punctuate the layout of a small garden or even act as an eye-catching centerpiece (see p.135 on positioning

Garden for pottering? *The relaxed intermingling of an assortment of pots amongst simple permanent planting has great charm.*

features). Containers are often the only feasible way of introducing planting into a confined or awkward space (see pp.168–71 for planting ideas).

The popular image of garden containers is of Mediterranean-style pots flooding over with colorful annuals. But there are many permutations in the relationship between pot and planting. Indeed the right pot with no planting at all can assume a sculptural quality. In the eighteenth century the boundaries between pot, plant and sculpture were deliberately blurred by the use of lead plants in those urns that were used as finials and the like.

When choosing a container ask yourself whether you want the pot, trough or tub to be of main interest rather than the plants you put in it? A lovely oil jar, for instance, can stand on its own without planting, providing visual pleasure in its shape. Or at the other extreme, do you need a pot

merely to hold earth, envisaging the plants as the main point of interest? Or perhaps you wish plant and pot to be of equal interest. Whatever the intended relationship of plant to pot is to be, it is important that the visual balance works.

Scale and style

Think also about how the shape and scale of your container will appear against its backdrop. Make sure that the style of your arrangement suits the mood of your garden. A jumble of pots can look very charming in the right environment – but beware, there is a very narrow dividing line between a jumble and a mess. A classical style urn, albeit made from reconstituted stone or fiberglass, is grand in style and may not be suited to a location which is humbler in feel. A pot which neither relates to the scale of a space, nor the overall style can ruin the total effect.

Materials

The natural materials from which containers are made include stone, reconstituted stone (stone which has been crushed, mixed with cement and/or resin and then molded), terracotta, wood, earthenware, and occasionally slate. Other materials that can look just as pleasing in the right place are concrete (possibly textured), metal and a wide range of man-made synthetics, including fiberglass and plastic.

Sculptural stone (above) *There is a medieval simplicity about this arrangement of unplanted containers, one of which is a disused font.*

Pool-side pots (below) *Here plants, pebbles and terracotta pots make an interesting arrangement of contrasting shape, color, and texture.*

Containers which are to be kept outside all year round in cold climates should be made from a frost-resistant material such as stone.

Happily, most plants can be grown in most types of pot, as long as the compost is correct and drainage adequate, so choose the pot which most suits the style of your garden and any envisaged planting. In a crisp modern setting you may well settle for the strong shapes of yuccas or cacti, best suited by a simply-shaped container.

Choosing a container

Though your choice may be tempered by economic considerations many people are willing to spend a relatively large amount of money on garden containers. It may well be worth splurging on a beautiful urn if it is to act as a permanent sculptural feature. However, why spend a lot on an imported Florentine pot only to conceal it with a mass of impatiens, when a far cheaper, simple terracotta pot will do the same job?

If you want a container that you can move about the garden or take inside during the winter bear in mind that its initial weight will be considerably increased by wet earth or compost. Incidentally, make sure that roofs and balconies are never overloaded with containers. Check with a structural engineer if you have any doubts. Where you must be careful of overloading, use lightweight plant containers and position them at the side, rather than in the middle of the roof, resting their weight on side walls when possible (but remember this may be dangerous if there are strong winds).

Positioning planted pots

As all plants are living, breathing things they need care. Make sure that you locate planted containers where there is enough light and where you can reach plants to look after them. Those on a hot roof, or exposed windowledge will require water maybe twice a day, perhaps justifying an automatic irrigation system, where practical.

Pleasing compositions *Placing a pale stone urn on a simple plinth against a vivid blue sky, right, makes for a stunning composition. The classical design of the urn is dramatically emphasized by the aloe's flower stalks.*

An alternative and more accessible use of an urn is shown below. Gentle herb planting complements the rounded forms of the container, which is shown to its best advantage against the neutral backdrop of a white fence.

FOCUS ON POTS

Pots and containers are an ideal way of enlivening the smallest and most awkward of spaces and, like those shown below, can make a dramatic, witty, or subtle statement. A single container might act as an eye-catching centerpiece or a group of planted pots as your doorstep mini-garden. Your choice of pot need by no means be limited to the purpose-made ones on the market, for plants can be grown in just about any receptacle (as long as you can make adequate drainage holes), which leaves plenty of scope for the inventive use of objects like chimney-pots, or even old boots.

In the Mediterranean and Mexico all sorts of cans, pots, and pans are colorfully planted and massed together, bringing color and interest to windowsills, doorways, alleyways and courtyards. Here is a selection of containers and planting of similar delight and ingenuity.

Strong shapes *This pair of handsome sculptured pots in terracotta is by Dina Princeloo. Spiky-leaved aloes complement rather than distract from their vigorous patterns.*

Chimney-pot planting *A solid-looking old pot and delicate planting of a pale pink fuchsia make a balanced contrast with a dramatic Rousseauesque mural on the wall behind.*

Saving space *Half this old Provençal oil jar has been sunk into a wall. Its curved form is unobscured by the simple planting of ivy-leaved geraniums (Pelargonium peltatum).*

Pots on plants *This group of unplanted ceramic pots clustered together against a clematis-covered wall makes a refreshing change to hanging baskets.*

Faded glory *Rich red flowers beckon the eye to this softly-colored urn which rests upon a pastel paved floor in a pool of gentle sunlight.*

Down to earth *Pairs of battered old boots sprouting with cacti and other succulents form a witty procession down the steps of this rambling cottage garden.*

SCULPTURAL FEATURES

A small-space garden needs a feature to act as a visual "punctuation mark" in the layout or as the culmination of the overall design. Water can do it, seating can do it and even people can do it, but when a garden has none of these you will have to be more inventive.

Choosing a feature

If the design is modern the feature might be sculpture, if traditional, statuary. For many it is a sort of half-way house that is sought, for sculpture is often too expensive, and statuary too grand. It might instead be a pot or a collection of pots like those shown below, a planted container, some boulders or a decorative wall plaque, a wall niche, or even the merest glimpse of a view, perhaps framed by a bogus shuttered window that you insert in a wall. Whatever your choice, it should both catch the eye and give a *raison d'être* to the structure of the garden or its planting.

Making a sculptural statement

Most of us tend to be very timid in our selection of external features, with the result that they do not make a strong enough statement within the

Sculptural pots (below) *Shadows from strong sunlight give added strength to this collection of sculptural pots by Dina Princeloo. Their bold shape contrasted against the niche is highlighted by the simple architectural planting.*

Eye-catching feature (above) *Sedums fill the palm of this sculpted outstretched hand to make a bold and handsome dual composition, which, positioned within luxuriant dark-green foliage, makes a compelling focus of interest.*

Sculpture garden (left) *This extraordinary selection of* objets trouvés *seen against a handsome green backdrop combines to create a fascinating tableau. The features create the garden's style rather than being a finishing touch.*

Decorative simplicity (below) *These two bronze cranes (sculpted by Robin Lewis) stand elegantly amongst two silver birch (Betula pendula). All are seen to striking effect against a simple backdrop.*

garden's design, or are swamped by plants. Often this is because an object is placed too low, so that it is not visible when sitting down inside.

Let its position be commanding, though not necessarily dominating, for half the secret of the correct siting of a feature outside is the way it is juxtaposed or counterbalanced with other objects, a tree perhaps, some seating, or even the view of a neighboring house.

Traditionally, a feature, usually a statue, was placed right in the middle of the garden, but few outside spaces today have the kind of symmetry which calls for this type of classical positioning. Placing a feature to one side of an area is one way of lending movement to a layout, however small.

Getting the scale right

Broadly speaking, the larger the object, the better it will do the job, for as well as providing a focal point within the garden it should focus the view from inside the house too. This is especially important when a space is too small, or awkwardly-placed to use, and serves just to be looked at through a door or from a window inside (see pp.36–7). Spotlit at night (drawings on p.136 show the different methods of lighting), an interesting sculptural feature outside will give your living space inside a whole new dimension and unify the whole inside/outside concept.

Choosing a feature

It is all too easy to choose a feature that is too small, position it in the garden and then, knowing that something is not quite right, add a pot near by, and then a specimen variegated shrub in an effort to bolster up its effect. The net result is that you draw attention to a disparate group of features and diminish the clarity of what you originally intended to be the eye-catcher.

Choosing a feature that is in the correct scale for its setting *is* difficult, since you do have to choose the object in isolation from its intended setting, so try to carry in your mind's eye an optimum height and breadth. This will help you to get the scale correct and ensure that your feature makes that vital visual punctuation mark.

LIGHTING

Outdoor lighting will maximize the pleasure you get from your small garden. It will enable you to eat, read, or simply putter about outside on warm spring and autumn evenings and, if you can see your garden from inside, enjoy a night-time view of it all year round, giving the room you are in (inside or outside) an extra dimension of space.

Outside lighting is essential in places where darkness falls early and the heat of the day makes escaping into the cool evening air a necessity. Even where summer evenings are long and light, subtle artificial lighting will enhance the atmosphere of a meal outside or a party on a terrace and enable you to use your outside space to the full when dusk turns to darkness.

Creative and functional lighting

Many people think of lighting a Christmas tree in the garden, but why stop there? Use lighting all the year round to create a gentle glow in the tracery of a fine specimen tree, to illuminate a group of pots, or to spotlight a piece of statuary,

even in winter and under snow. Make the most of whatever features you have, especially if they are in a space you cannot actually use. If you live in the country, lighting will give you a hint of the wildness beyond your own small patch. Other sorts of lighting have primarily a functional rather than decorative purpose: such as that between the garage and the front door, alongside a flight of steps, or brilliant security lighting.

Creating the effect you want

Each of these types of lighting needs a different treatment. First, decide on exactly what you want lit and the sort of effect you are after. Be practical – appealing as subtle half-lighting might be, if you are barbecuing or pouring a drink, you will end up in a mess. For this sort of activity and for lighting paths and steps you need a direct source of light. Position the light fitting near the area you want lit, but low to avoid creating an eerie effect; bulkhead fittings let into walls do the trick perfectly. For eating outside or reading you can

Giving a clear view *The whole garden space is illuminated by a powerful spotlight positioned high up on the house. This method of lighting will give a good view of the garden space from inside the house, but anyone actually in the garden would find themselves dazzled by it.*

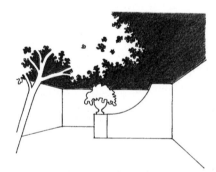

Dramatic light and shadow *The light source is screened by the dividing wall, creating an exciting theatrical effect when seen from inside the house. Additional lighting, in the form of small lamps or candles, would be needed if the foreground area were to be used for cooking or eating outside.*

Subtle overall illumination *A light under the tree points upwards, illuminating the branches and creating enough light to make the whole of the space usable. To create different effects use a combination of the two methods of lighting that are illustrated above.*

use a simple outdoor table lamp. Install water-proofed sockets in different places so you can move the light around.

For special occasions there is nothing more pleasing than the gentle flicker of candlelight; this combined with indoor lighting may be all you need to illuminate a small space near the house.

Light fittings and installation

Choose light fittings that are practical and suit the style of your outside room; if in doubt choose a simple, strong, and unobtrusive design. It is vital that you use light fittings specially designed for outside use and that they are professionally wired and installed. It is simplest to use the internal mains circuit for lighting a small space near the home, rather than going to the trouble of installing a separate garden circuit. All light fittings, cables and powerpoints must be waterproofed and wrapped where they might be damaged by a fork or spade when gardening.

Night-time effects (left and below) *A spotlight illuminates the Gothic arch, left, while interior lighting in combination with external fittings give the narrow decked area, below, a warm glow.*

FABRICS

In a large space the impact of chair covers, cushions, umbrellas, and awnings is diluted by the amount of vegetation and space that lies between them. In a small garden space, however, fabrics really come into their own, giving a sense of softness and luxury that makes up for the lack of vegetation and creating a comfortable and inviting room-like environment.

Structures and furnishings

A fabric "ceiling", in the form of an awning, will either shade you from the sun or enable you to be outside, oblivious to the gray skies overhead and, if you are overlooked from above, it will give you privacy too. Small standard-shaped awnings, either designed to be attached to a wall at one end or to be supported by a frame and thus free-standing, can be bought in kit form. If your space is awkwardly-shaped you may need to design or make your own (see p.198 for construction details). A swag awning can be made by attaching fabric to the underside of a pergola's horizontals.

Large umbrellas make ideal portable, temporary "ceilings" for small gardens. They can be positioned in just the right place over a table or sunbathing bed and are easily folded up and stored away. Vertical "walls" of fabric will give you privacy from neighbor's gardens and shelter from side winds (see p.198).

Luxurious setting *The ivory-colored awning creates a softly-lit setting with an air of luxury enhanced by subtly-colored soft furnishings.*

Chair covers, cushions, rugs, and tablecloths are all possible seasonal additions to your outside space and can have more impact than plants. Taken outside on a sunny day and grouped around a rug, large cushions will transform your balcony, rooftop, or ground-level garden into an inviting and comfortable room in which to relax.

Choosing fabrics

Fabrics for outside use should be tough (and preferably washable) and suit the style of your garden space. Patterned fabrics hide the dirt better than plain ones and so are particularly useful in dusty towns and cities.

Take fabric samples outside and visualize what they will look like there in the form of a chair cover or umbrella in relation to the colors of your garden's structures and other "furnishings".

A hard-working fabric, such as canvas or sailcloth, should be used for the weatherside of awnings; the underside can be lined, or softly swagged with a more delicate fabric for an exotic tented effect – think of the colorful awnings with braiding and mirrored inlay depicted in Indian and Persian paintings.

Canvas screens (above and left) *Canvas attached to metal frames has been used to make a side and overhead screen for a small, city roof-space. The triangular side screen, above, provides privacy and shelter from side drafts, and the overhead screen, left, shades part of the roof-space from the sun.*

Practical style (right) *These robust, canvas umbrellas, arranged to make a sculptural composition, are both practical and stylish. Umbrellas make excellent portable shelters from the sun or light rain, and occupy a small amount of storage space.*

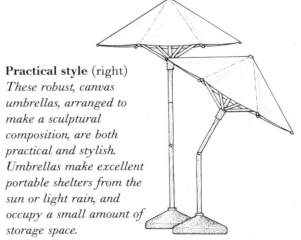

FREE-STANDING FURNITURE

Whatever the size of your garden, its furniture should be an integral part of your whole design, rather than an afterthought. But when space is limited it is especially important to think about furniture from the planning stage onwards.

So ask yourself plenty of questions. Do you ever work or write outside? Do you need furniture that can withstand being used by children as an adventure playground? Or would you like a bench where you can briefly pause in the shade, or a table near the kitchen door so you can prepare food in the fresh air?

Relating shapes

The way in which the shape and bulk of a grouping of furniture, or a single bench, relates to the rest of the garden is as important as how you plan the massing of plant material. Both are part of the balance of the garden. Consider not only the practical aspects of your furniture, but also how its style suits that of your garden and house, and the impact of its shape and color.

It is important to decide whether your furniture will be in the garden all the year round, in which case it will in effect be a permanent part of the garden's structure, or if its presence will be temporary, maybe there for just a few months or the odd day. Furniture which is a permanent fixture should have a settled look and a bulk and stability in scale with its surroundings. Often the most satisfactory way of achieving this is by having built-in furniture (see p.144 for design ideas). An eye-catching piece of garden furniture can become a sculptural feature in its own right and perhaps inspire your choice of materials and other aspects of your garden's design.

Furniture that is outside for limited periods should not give the appearance of ill-considered clutter. Make sure, too, that an area such as a terrace where furniture is temporarily arranged for entertaining does not look neglected and unwelcoming when cleared. Try to visualize what your garden space will look like without, as well as with, furniture.

Big color blocks
(below) *You can use pieces of furniture to juxtapose bold shapes in a small space.*

Chic metal (right)
The lines of this black, metal furniture echo the filigreed pattern of the trees' branches above.

Comfort and practicality on the one hand and stylish design on the other need not be mutually exclusive, though to look at much garden furniture on the market this might seem so. It is worth hunting around for pieces that are functional as well as aesthetically pleasing. Violently-colored hectically-patterned upholstery may look fine in brilliant sunshine or against an azure sea, but out of place and gaudy in a gray-skied suburban garden. Always consider how the color of your furniture is affected by the quality of natural light in your garden.

Choosing a style

So what is the ideal? Furniture constructed from natural materials and upholstered in neutral colors, tends to fit more comfortably with natural forms, as do curving organic shapes. However, the "natural" look may not necessarily be in keeping with the location of your outside space, the architecture of your house or the style of its interior decor and furnishing.

You will see, below, that every material has its own character, and it may be that the hard look of a sleek metal chair suits the feel of your urban balcony and echoes the chic style of the room from which it leads.

Furniture as a visual link

If a beautifully designed and constructed chair is the key to linking interior and exterior it is worth the investment. In a limited space the visual connection between the two is particularly important. The division between them can either be softened by having furniture which is akin in style to that inside, or by linking the two in the color or texture of upholstery. When arranging furniture outside it is important to consider what it will look like from inside too.

Ensuring comfort

Choose furniture which suits its function as well as being good to look at. A chair used for sitting at a table for meals should not only provide back support and be at a suitable height and angle to the table, but should be comfortable enough to loll in, for summer lunches and terrace dinners can be memorable occasions to linger over. Ornate iron and look-a-like aluminum seating seldom provides this comfort, unlike canvas-seated director's chairs, or pine kitchen furniture.

For reading the Sunday papers or a book outside bucket-shaped chairs are perfect; even swing settees (though to my mind hideous contraptions) impossible to hide in winter, are undeniably comfortable. Lightweight, folding chairs, though easily stored and ideal for impromptu seating, are completely unsuited to true sybaritic pleasure. Sunbathing beds, such as those found on French

Natural colors *The fresh white of this neat row of wicker chairs makes a pleasing contrast with the warm terracotta paintwork. The green trim around the seats echoes the rich greens of the shutters behind, and the grass.*

and Italian beaches are practical, comfortable and attractive, unlike those, with wheels and handles and collapsable back rests, which require masses of storage space and feats of patient endurance to click into position. The lines of a small swimming pool are far better suited by simple furniture than that which is "fussy" and cumbersome.

Try to find garden furniture which suits the style of your life. To my mind, much that is available may not do so, swinging as it does between self-conscious elegance on the one hand and rustic "olde-worlde" charm on the other.

Materials

Well-seasoned wood will last a life-time and withstand hot sun, rain, and frost. It is also the easiest material to use for making your own furniture. Left natural and finished with a clear preservative it blends in well with the natural forms of a garden. Painted, it can add a new dimension, and bring out the color of a neighboring wall or door.

Metal takes kindly to modern design, though not to the damp. Unless it is plastic coated it will require regular repainting to prevent it becoming rusty and looking neglected. Plastic, on the other hand, requires no maintenance, is practical for all climates, and light, so makes ideal portable furniture, but unlike a material such as stone, does not weather pleasingly with age.

Blissful retreat *This informal arrangement of cushions on an oriental rug exudes an air of relaxation and gives this private retreat an unexpected* indoor quality. The dappled greens of nature and the browns of the wicker basket and stool tone well with the neutral color of the cushions.

Slatted bench *The color and fluid forms of the bench and the planting combine to create an inviting spot to look at or sit in.*

Purity of color *The central placing of this simple white wooden bench draws the eye through an elegant drift of golden-yellow* Coreopsis verticillata.

BUILT-IN FURNITURE

Building furniture into the structure of your garden is an effective way of making the most of the space you have, both visually and physically. The most important advantage, visually, is that furniture which is treated as an integral part of the overall design (constructed from a material which blends in well with surrounding structures) gives a small area a unified look that makes it appear larger. Built-in furniture also helps avoid the clutter often created by free-standing chairs and tables and solves the problem of where to store them. Even the smallest free-standing table with a chair on either side needs a minimum 2m (6 ft) of clear space – this is a considerable amount in a very cramped site.

Using existing features

Existing features can be modified to make seating space, or new features designed so they have a dual function. Raising the wall around an existing pool, for instance, will provide you with an area on which to sit or stand pots. Retaining walls around a bed can be designed so they are at a suitable height for casual seating. Raised brick or concrete slabs ("pads") designed as a permanent part of a garden's pattern can be used as a low table or for seating; when not in use they will blend in naturally with the rest of the garden.

Trees and play areas

Existing trees, which often occupy rather high proportions of space in a small garden, can be used to save space at ground level, by being used as a support for a hammock, for example, or light fixtures. Large trees can be turned to good use for children; they can become home to a tree house or used to support a swing, rope-ladder or knotted length of rope. Play features like this can easily be dismantled when the children grow older. When building a play area with a more permanent structure, it is wise to have an alternative use in mind for later years. A raised sand-pit, for example, could be used later as a water feature and its walls as casual seating.

Materials

To create a unified look choose materials that complement the rest of the garden. If using wood, choose a hardwood, for softwoods tend to splinter. Concrete is cheap and durable, but austere. Its appearance can be softened, however, by hanging plants, for example, or by combining another material such as wood. Brick is one of the most useful materials, for its small unit size makes it is possible to build furniture in awkward spaces.

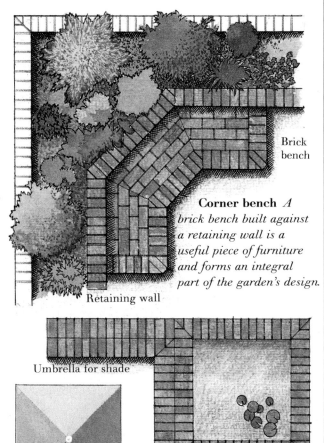

Brick bench

Corner bench *A brick bench built against a retaining wall is a useful piece of furniture and forms an integral part of the garden's design.*

Retaining wall

Umbrella for shade

Casual seating

Waterside seating *The walls around this pool have been raised to a height suitable for casual seating. This feature could also be used as a sand-pit, but should be covered with mesh when not in use to protect it from marauding cats.*

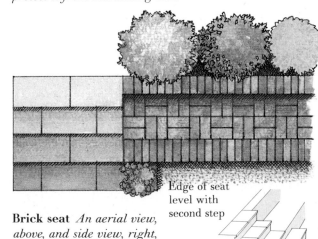

Edge of seat level with second step

Brick seat *An aerial view, above, and side view, right, of a built-in brick seat that echoes the shape of the adjoining flight of steps.*

PLANTING

The sheer number of garden plants on offer
can make selecting those which suit both the
location and style of your space seem a
daunting prospect.

This planting guide spans from how to plan
your scheme and make creative combinations
of shape, color and texture to choosing a
shrub for a windswept balcony or a scented
climber to clothe a pergola.

GARDEN SOFTWARE

Though I agree with Thomas Church's philosophy that "gardens are for people", plants are important too, for they help your outside room to become your breathing space – a place to escape from the pressures of everyday life. The sight, sounds and smells of plants are a great restorative and, for many people, tending them is wonderfully relaxing.

Plants, that are used to enhance the style and mood of your outside space, should be treated as an integral part of its design – the shape of your bed or arrangement of planted containers, for instance, should relate to the scale of a paved area and the colors of your plants to surrounding colors. It is a myth that small spaces need peppering with small details and ornate, miniaturized planting schemes – quite the reverse – bold, simple planting schemes created from a limited range of plant material are nearly always the most effective.

Plant design is about manipulating multiple quantities of plant material. Do not attempt to dive in at the deep end and try to create a border worthy of Gertrude Jekyll at the first attempt. One of the joys of planting is seeing the right balance develop, and moving plants around each autumn as you seek to create the wonderful image you hold in your mind's eye.

Strong shapes (above)
The strength of this scheme lies in the arrangement of strong, linear plant shapes.

Dramatic color (right)
A small range of yellow and green plants combines to make an eye-catching composition.

PLANNING YOUR PLANTING

Many gardeners, small-space or otherwise, are content for their garden to be a collection of their favorite plants, "arranged" in a queue. But your carefully planned structure deserves plants that suit its scale and will act as the catalyst to bring your garden to life.

Choosing plants

To begin with, only use plants you are familiar with – look them up in a catalogue or directory, and check the "feel" of them at a nursery or garden center. This may well limit you to a small range of material, but this is all to the good, as too much variety of plant form and shape can lead to a staccato, "liquorice-all-sorts" effect, instead of the harmonious blend of plant forms and colors you should be seeking to create. The next step is to classify your plant material, working down in scale from the largest to the smallest.

Feature plants and skeleton plants

First, decide what your key plants or "specials" are going to be. These can be used as a visual link between your planting and the surrounding architecture, for instance a weeping cherry curving over a pool wall. On a smaller scale, the "special" might be a yucca acting as an evergreen pivot in a group of perennials. You could even have a major and a minor "special", counter-balancing one another within the overall design.

Next choose your skeleton planting. This should be evergreen so it provides a permanent structure and background to the rest of your plants and its bulk reinforces the overall design of your garden, screening and providing shelter (for you and your plants) where necessary.

It is important to plan ahead when planting, particularly in the case of evergreen shrubs, many of which take a long time to mature. Try to envisage how the plants will look in five years' time rather than next year, and space them accordingly. If you make a plan of your garden and shade in the evergreens, you will have a clear idea of the space left. You can always use quick infillers to fill in the gaps while the skeleton planting matures (see pp.156–9 for "instant" plants).

Decorative infill

Having selected your skeleton plants, you can start to think about the style or mood you want your planting scheme to have and to choose seasonally decorative shrubs (again working down in scale from large to small). Group shrubs so they are in scale with the design of your garden; the width of the terrace they border, for instance, or the height of a fence or tree behind them. Avoid using too many single decorative infill plants; they might detract from the effectiveness of the "specials".

The "pretties"

The next step is to choose what I call "pretties". Into this category come smaller shrubby species such as *Santolina* spp., some *Hebe* spp., all the perennials and many herbs. Unless working on the tiniest scale, these should be planted in masses as well, with an eye to the way the texture and color of their foliage in particular (this outlasts flower color) relates to the plants around them. Finally, consider infillers: bulbs such as tulips and irises, self-seeding biennials, annuals such as impatiens and ground cover plants like hostas and ajuga all come into this category.

Making a planting plan *Your planting scheme should be conceived in relation to your overall design and used to soften and overlay its hard structures. The best way to plan your planting is to indicate the position and approximate spread of fully-matured plants on a scaled plan. The planting plan shown here is for the garden used as an example in the section on planning your space (see pp.62–7).*

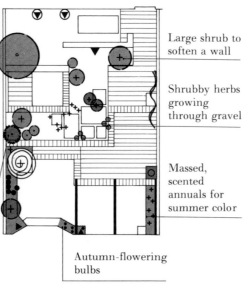

Large shrub to soften a wall

Shrubby herbs growing through gravel

Massed, scented annuals for summer color

Evergreen shrub for year-round shape

Autumn-flowering bulbs

Using symbols *You can use the symbols shown below to represent different categories of plant material.*

▲ Climber

∴ Bulbs

++ Small infill plants

☁ Evergreen

🌣 Deciduous shrub

◯ Tree

Silver and gray scheme There are many plants with gray and silver foliage and they can be combined to create a scheme with a light, airy atmosphere. Their intensity of color varies according to the texture and density of their foliage, and they can be arranged so that some parts of a scheme have an ethereal quality and others a bold appearance.

The key plant in this scheme is the yucca. Its sharp, sculptural shape is balanced by the rounded form of two gray *Ozothamnus* spp. Foliage ranges from light silver to gray-green.

Flower colors are linked too – the yellow daisy-flowers of *Senecio laxifolius* with those of the yellow-centered *Anthemis cupaniana* and the purple flowers of the silver-leaved *Erysimum* sp. with the gentle pink blooms of *Ozothamnus* sp.

The overall look
(above) *In a small space it is the variety of textures of gray and silver foliage that makes a year-round impact.*

Planting out (left)
These plants (and those overleaf) were arranged in small, square beds. The result, two years later, is shown above.

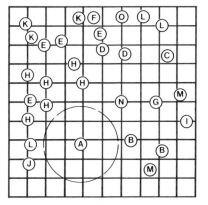

A *Yucca* sp.
B *Senecio laxifolius*
C *Ozothamnus* sp.
D *Artemesia* 'Powis Castle'
E *Ruta graveolens* 'Jackman's Blue'
F *Achillea filipendulina* 'Gold Plate'
G *Verbascum bombyciferum*
H *Erysimum variegatum*
I *Hosta tokudama*
J *Hedera helix*
K *Lamium maculatum*
L *Anthemis cupaniana*
M *Digitalis grandiflora*
N *Senecio* sp.
O *Artemesia* sp.

Purple scheme Purple is a demanding color (more usual in foliage than flower) and difficult to incorporate within a mixed group. However, an arrangement of varying shades of purple has a spectacular effect and creates a moody atmosphere.

Of the few evergreen, purple-foliaged shrubs, most belong to the *Berberis* genus. In this scheme *B. gagnepainii* 'Wallichiana Purpurea' and purple elder (*Sambucus nigra* 'Purpurea') are used as a backing to the huge leaves of *Ligularia dentata* 'Desdemona'. Fennel (*Foeniculum vulgare*) makes a soft, feathery contrast with the firm, fleshy leaves of *Sedum maximum* 'Atropurpureum'.

The ground-cover infillers that complement the rest of a scheme include the bronzy-purple *Ajuga reptans* 'Atropurpurea' and *Saxifraga* sp.

The overall look (above) *Rich tones and a strong contrast of shapes and textures give this purple scheme a highly dramatic flavor.*

Planting out (left) *The plants that will become the dramatic focal points of this composition look small and unassuming at the planting stage.*

A *Sambucus nigra* 'Purpurea'
B *Weigela* sp.
C *Ligularia dentata* 'Desdemona'
D *Berberis gagnepainii* 'Wallichiana Purpurea'
E *Foeniculum vulgare*
F *Sedum* 'Ruby Mantle'
G *Saxifraga* sp.
H *Ajuga reptans* 'Atropurpurea'
I *Euphorbia amygdaloides robbiae*
J *Erysimum linifolium* 'Bowles Mauve'
K *Sedum maximum* 'Atropurpureum'

Gold and yellow scheme Gold is a warm and sunny color that will brighten any area, even on a dull day. Gold foliage combines well with green, cream, lemon, and yellow flower colors – blue could be added for a touch of excitement.

Two variegated flag irises (*Iris pseudacorus*) are the dramatic focal point of this scheme. Their strong, vertical form contrasts with the small-leaved shrubs *Lonicera nitida* 'Baggesen's Gold' and *Symphoricarpos orbiculatus* 'Variegatus', which form a gentle golden backdrop and bulk out the composition. Golden elder (*Sambucus nigra* 'Aurea') and gold *Physocarpus* sp. give height and their well-defined leaf shapes are a background to a soft mass of golden sage (*Salvia* sp.). Summer color includes foxgloves and feverfew.

The overall look (above) *The color and texture of foliage, which forms the basis of the scheme, is complemented by seasonal flower color.*

Planting out (left) *The permanent plants were arranged so there is room for annuals and bulbs for seasonal flower color.*

A *Iris pseudacorus*
B *Lonicera nitida* 'Baggesen's Gold'
C *Sambucus nigra* 'Aurea'
D *Physocarpus* sp.
E *Symphoricarpos orbiculatus* 'Variegatus'
F *Euonymus fortunei* 'Emerald 'n' Gold'
G *Hypericum × inodorum* 'Ysella'
H *Sedum spectabile* 'Variegatum'
I *Chrysanthemum parthenium*
J *Digitalis grandiflora*
K *Melissa officinalis* 'Aurea'
L *Salvia officinalis* 'Icterina'
M *Primula bulleyana*
N *Lysimachia nummularia*

VERTICAL PLANTING

Climbers are invaluable in the small-space garden. Not only do they make it possible to enjoy plants for their own sake, without using up valuable ground space, but they can be used to soften visually hard structures or disguise ugly ones and, in conjunction with a pergola or openwork fencing, provide privacy, shade and shelter.

Types of climbers

Some climbers, such as ivy (*Hedera* spp.), have sucker-like roots that attach themselves to vertical surfaces and require no additional form of support. Others, such as sweet peas (*Lathyrus odoratus*) and *Clematis* spp., have small tendrils that twist and twine around a support such as trelliswork, openwork fencing or a host plant.

In addition to these true climbers there are plants, like *Cotoneaster horizontalis*, which will push themselves up a vertical surface, without occupying much ground space. These can be contrasted with those that hang downwards – the most effective softeners of boundary walls, such as *Cotoneaster dammeri*. Many shrubs which are perfectly at home in the open, such as *Magnolia grandiflora* will, if supported and pruned into shape, happily grow tall and upright when planted against a vertical surface. Different types of climber are illustrated in detail on page 202.

Supporting climbers

Trelliswork and wires can be used to support climbers; wires provide the most imperceptible support (see p.195 for construction details), but are not suitable for heavy climbers. Trelliswork can be used purely as a plant support, in which case it should dominate neither the wall nor the plant, or as a decorative feature in its own right, the plant acting merely as a cosmetic softener, in which case it should be eye-catching, perhaps painted a bright color or large in relation to the scale of the plant.

Vertical garden
A variety of climbers have transformed this small entrance area into a lush vertical garden. Ivy (Hedera *sp.) forms the evergreen base, contrasted by the grey rosettes of* Echeveria *sp. To the side grows jasmine* (Trachelospermum jasminoides) *and around the door a fruiting vine* (Vitis *sp.).*

ENGLISH IVY
Hedera helix 'Goldheart'

English ivy is one of the most useful evergreens for covering small vertical surfaces (Persian ivy (*H. colchica*), which has large leaves, becomes too rampant). 'Goldheart' grows well in shade and will brighten up walls in dingy corners.

BOSTON IVY
Parthenocissus tricuspidata

For autumn color the brilliant foliage of Boston ivy cannot be excelled. It will grow vigorously up walls of any aspect, to a height of 7.5–15m (25–50 ft), and because it is tolerant of atmospheric pollution is particularly suitable for town and city gardens. *P. quinquefolia* cultivars also have bright foliage.

CHILEAN POTATO TREE
Solanum crispum 'Glasnevin'

The purple-blue blooms of *Solanum crispum* last from early summer to mid-autumn, so will give a small garden-space a long-lasting splash of color without using up valuable ground space. If supported it will grow quite tall. Not hardy in cold climates.

SCARLET TRUMPET HONEYSUCKLE
Lonicera brownii 'Dropmore Scarlet'

With support, most varieties of honeysuckle (except the shrubby honeysuckles) will grow up walls, fences and pergolas, and around doors and windows. The unscented variety 'Dropmore Scarlet' bears a profusion of brilliantly-colored flowers between spring and late summer. It grows best in light shade.

KOLOMIKTA VINE
Actinidia kolomikta

COMMON HOP
Humulus lupulus 'Aureus'

This golden-yellow hop has a phenomenal annual growth of up to 10m (33 ft), so is ideal for giving a small garden a lush green appearance in a short time, while taking up very little ground space. It will grow happily on walls of all aspects.

CEANOTHUS
Ceanothus × *delilianus*

Fragrant, powder-blue flowers adorn *Ceanothus* × *delilianus* 'Gloire de Versailles' from mid-summer until autumn. It has a shrubby growth habit and needs to be trained to cover vertical surfaces. Most species and forms, known as California-lilac in western USA, are not hardy in cold climates.

The tips of *Actinidia kolomikta*'s green leaves look as if they have been gently dipped in pink and white paint. Trained on wires, it will cover walls with an elegant mass of pastel-colored foliage until its leaves fall in autumn. The leaves are most colorful when the plant is mature and grown in full sun.

FREMONTODENDRON
Fremontodendron 'California Glory'

CLIMBING ROSE
Rosa 'Mme. Alfred Carrière'

The fragrant blooms of climbing roses will give just as much pleasure as those of shrub roses, without using up as much ground-level space. *R.* 'Mme. Alfred Carrière' is resistant to atmospheric pollution so is especially suitable for city spaces.

DWARF MORNING GLORY
Convolvulus 'Tricolor'

The stunning deep-purple, yellow-centered flowers of this annual climber provide a brilliant splash of color from mid-summer through to early autumn. It will climb a trellis or wire support with ease, like its close relatives (*Ipomoea* spp. and cvs.) such as 'Heavenly Blue' and 'Scarlett O'Hara'.

This shrub can be planted out in a container if you have no bed, and trained up any sheltered vertical surface which gets plenty of sun. Its coarse, gray-green leaves are an excellent foil for its bright-yellow, single flowers which bloom from late spring to late summer. A western US native, not hardy in cold areas.

INSTANT PLANTING

"Instant" plants are those which have a rapid yearly growth and thus have an immediate impact on the area in which they are planted. All annuals come into this category, as do some biennials and fast-growing shrubs and climbers.

Short-term impact

There can be gaps in even the most thoughtfully organized planting arrangements, and in such cases annuals are indispensable. There are many other situations where annuals are useful too. For example, many small urban spaces, such as roofs and windowsills, rely entirely on annuals as a source of color, particularly where conditions are too harsh for shrubs to overwinter. They are also useful for people who live in houses for short seasonal periods and want a quick, colorful effect.

Longer term infilling

Annuals are also useful for those who are trying to establish a long-term tree and shrub grouping, where fillers are needed to thicken out slower growing material. For quick infills at a lower level use pot marigolds (*Calendula* spp.) and forget-me-nots (*Myosotis* spp.). Evergreens take a particularly long time to establish; in this situation fast-growing deciduous shrubs with a relatively short life span such as broom (*Cytisus* spp.) can be used as long-term infillers and moved when appropriate. Sunflowers (*Helianthus* cvs.) and annual climbers such as runner beans, morning glory, hop (*Humulus lupulus*) and the cup-and-saucer plant (*Cobaea scandens*) are ideal for giving seasonal height to a maturing planting scheme or providing a temporary screen while a hedging plant (such as box or yew) grows.

Biennials

Using biennials in the role of instant plants requires a little more forward planning, for they need to be planted one year to flower the next. Those which reach a considerable height include foxgloves (*Digitalis* spp.) and *Verbascum* spp.

A bold arrangement *If you want to combine brightly-colored annuals, be bold and flamboyant about it, and arrange them in strong masses against a simple background, like the dark green shrubs here.*

TOBACCO PLANT
Nicotiana × sanderae

The tobacco plant is an extremely useful annual, for it grows quickly to a height of approximately 1m (3 ft) during the summer, and makes an excellent infiller for a sunny space. *N. × s.* 'Domino Mixed', has a wonderful, heady scent.

COMMON ELDER
Sambucus nigra

The garden forms of the common elder (*Sambucus nigra*) are quick-growing shrubs, which can be cut down each autumn for extra spring vigor. Variegated, gold, and purple forms exist, and their leaf shapes and sizes vary considerably.

BUTTERFLY BUSH
Buddleia davidii 'Peace'

The butterfly bush grows up to 3m (10 ft) in a season. It is excellent for filling in space in a new planting of slow-growing evergreens; just remove it after five years or so. To achieve maximum growth cut back hard after flowering.

NASTURTIUM
Tropaeolum majus nanum

Nasturtiums are extremely fast-growers, either trailing along the ground, or climbing up a surface. 'Jewel Mixed' has lovely clear-colored flowers, which bloom from early summer through to autumn, and simple foliage. Their only drawback is that in an enclosed space they tend to attract aphids.

SUNFLOWER
Helianthus annuus

Sunflowers are giant, daisy-like flowers that thrive in full sun. They can grow to more than 3m (10 ft) in height and their flowers are often as much as 30cm (1 ft) wide. As they attain these dimensions in just a season they make ideal infillers or temporary screens. The most common flower color is gold.

RUSSIAN VINE
Polygonum baldschuanicum

NEMESIA
Nemesia strumosa

WARMINSTER BROOM
Cytisus × praecox

For an "instant" screen use Russian vine. It is extremely vigorous and can grow up to 3m (10 ft) in a year, but before planting bear in mind that it will spread at the same rate over the years. Sprays of white flowers last from mid-summer until autumn.

The mixed colors of the cultivar 'Triumph Mixed' create a cheerful, cottage garden mood. All cultivars of this annual flower best in soil which is fertile and moist, so if growing in a container use moisture-retentive soil.

If Warminster broom is cut back with shears after flowering, its silky green shoots will make rapid growth during the next season, making it an ideal shrub to infill a slower growing group of evergreen shrubs. It is resistant to polluted air.

IMPATIENS
Impatiens walleriana 'Red Star'

PASSION FLOWER
Passiflora caerulea

Impatiens are usually treated as annuals and bear a profusion of flowers from spring to autumn, so can be used as a quick colorful infillers in a mixed scheme. They are ideal for planting in all types of containers and will grow in sun or light shade, so can also be used to provide "instant" color.

The passion flower has a rapid rate of growth and its evergreen leaves make a handsome year-round screen, enhanced by its summer display of exotic flowers.

It will cling to a lattice or wire support by means of tendrils and, as it can be planted in containers, can be grown in any location which is in sun or light shade.

FOXGLOVE
Digitalis purpurea

Foxgloves are biennial or perennial and grow 1–1.5m (3–5 ft); in summer they produce bell-shaped blooms, and, as a whole, bring height and color to a planting scheme in a minimum of time. They grow well in moist soil in sun or shade and selfsow.

STOCK
Matthiola 'Giant Excelsior'

Stocks are traditional cottage garden plants with soft coloring and a heady scent. They flower in summer and make gentle-looking infillers for a small mixed scheme; they are also excellent for cutting, so their fragrance can be appreciated inside too. There is a large range of biennial and annual cultivars.

POT MARIGOLD
Calendula officinalis

Pot marigolds are one of the easiest annuals to grow and their firm, bright blooms lend themselves to a variety of garden moods. This cultivar 'Fiesta Gitana' is smaller than many others, and has a lower, more spreading shape.

SWEET ALYSSUM
Lobularia maritima

Sweet alyssum, though actually a perennial, is often grown as an annual and is a popular garden plant, for it has small leaves, a dense mounded growth and a profusion of flowers which last right through from early spring until the first frosts of autumn. It looks attractive when grown between the cracks in paving.

PLANTS FOR COLOR

Color is a rejuvenator and revives the spirits, and many urban dwellers use brightly-colored planting as a relief from the monotonous grays and browns around them. When choosing plants, consider not only the temporary flamboyance of annual flower color, but the more permanent displays of foliage, stem, branch and bark. Foliage colors range from all the many shades of green, through to gold, bronze, purple and silver, while stem and branch colors include yellows, greens, browns and reds. These should be combined to create year-round displays that will provide a foil to seasonal flower color.

Linking color

Whether your garden consists of a few pots on a balcony or a few planters in a basement entrance, try to tailor your range of plants so their color blends well with the surroundings. You have to remember that every element in a limited space, from walls and paving to chair-cover fabric, will be seen in unison. Peppering a small space with many contrasted colors that have no link to one another or their surroundings will create a random, disparate appearance; creating a harmonious composition by linking colors will unify your space and make it appear larger.

The impact of color

The impact of the color of each plant in a scheme will vary according to its size, so when planning a scheme bear in mind the dimensions to which each plant will grow and how this will effect the distribution of different colors.

Try to visualize the effect of shade or brilliant sunshine on different colors for this can radically alter their effect. Red, for instance, is a demanding color that is hard to use outside, especially in bright sun, but in a shaded area can be combined effectively with gray, purples and pinks.

Color combination
Pale-mauve Petunia *cv. with* Lobelia *cv., gray* Helichrysum petiolatum *and* Chrysanthemum × superbum *make a stunning combination against a bright-blue door. In a small space, where you are unlikely to be able to contrast many plants against a natural backdrop, look to the color of surrounding structures for inspiration.*

WINGED SPINDLE TREE
Euonymus alata

The dark green leaves of this deciduous shrub turn to a brilliant red in the autumn, when they are accompanied by small, purple and red fruits. It grows slowly to a height of 2.5m (8 ft) so is perfect for small garden spaces.

RED-BARKED DOGWOOD
Cornus alba 'Sibirica'

The coral-red stems of *Cornus alba* 'Sibirica' are stunning in bright winter light. The most intensive color is in the young wood, so cut back the stems in spring before its leaves appear; it will grow up to 1.8m (6 ft) tall so cutting back will also prevent it becoming too large for a small garden area.

TULIP
Tulipa 'Queen of Night'

Few plants have such an extraordinary depth of color as *Tulipa* 'Queen of Night'. Its bronzy-black petals have a luxurious satin-like quality and will add a touch of mysterious splendor to the smallest of garden spaces.

LILY-FLOWERED TULIP
Tulipa 'White Triumphator'

For an unusual combination of color, contrast this pure-white lily-flowered tulip with the gorgeous bronzy-black foliage of *Tulipa* 'Queen of Night'.

FLOWERING CABBAGE
Brassica oleracea

For a dramatic display grow the purple-bronze *Coleus blumei* 'Autumn Splendour' around an exuberantly-patterned cream and green decorative cabbage.

COLOR CHOICE

Choosing plants that combine to create a harmonious color composition, rather than a strongly contrasting one, will give the smallest areas unity, and, therefore, the biggest sense of space. So try to make a controlled selection from the myriad of plant colors available. The arrangement on this page consists of warm tones of orange and pink and a strong yellow, with splashes of cream and a dash of pure white which prevent it becoming aggressively hot. To have introduced blue, for instance, would have disrupted the whole scheme. If you do not wear every color under the sun at one time, or decorate a room in a jumble of colors, why plant that way?

It is the injudicious use of annual flower color that so often spoils a display. Try to avoid using 'mixed' shades (so heavily promoted in plant catalogues) for these often consist of garish combinations that serve only to disrupt an otherwise harmonious composition.

The effects of color

Choose a combination of colors that suits the mood of your garden space. You may have a basement yard with a dark, mysterious atmosphere that would be strengthened by the use of deep greens, maroons, and bronzes. On a cool, airy terrace, on the other hand, fresh creams, pinks and silvers would be complementary. To see the effect different colors have upon one another, arrange pieces of card in different combinations. Some colors are more versatile than others. Lemon, for example, can be warmed up with yellow and orange, or cooled down with pale blue, gray and white. Once you have a scheme that you find pleasing, make your selection of plants.

Balanced color *Tones of yellow, pink, cream and orange have here been combined to create a harmonious composition. The warm tones, which reach a peak in strong, hot yellows, are all cooled by a splash of crisp white, which gives the display a refreshing "breather".*

Connecting pink Soft pink, in the form of a *Pelargonium zonale* cultivar links with the warm tones of the tall lilies at the rear of the display.

Harmony The magnificent apricot flower of this *Hibiscus* hybrid contains elements of the colors of its immediate neighbors.

Cream link The cream flowers of a begonia contrast with the crisp white blooms of its neighbor and complement the warm tones of the rest of the scheme.

Warm and strong The warm tones of the rest of the arrangement reach a peak in the orange of *Lilium* 'Enchantment' and yellow blooms of *Lilium* 'Golden Clarion'.

Cooling white The strong yellows of the tall *Chrysanthemum frutescens* 'Aurea' and the foreground begonia are cooled by the white *Pelargonium* cv.

PLANTING FOR SCENT

There is nothing quite as alluring and luxurious as scent – something no small garden need ever be without, for many scented plants are climbers, so take up little ground space, or can be planted in containers and thus enjoyed in any location. The smaller your space the closer to your scented plants you will be, and the more enclosed it is the more intense their fragrance.

Scented plants can be enjoyed outside, and from inside, through an open door or window; so why not get extra pleasure from them by planting roses around your bedroom window, aromatic herbs in a tub on your kitchen windowsill or fragrant lilies in a container on your doorstep? Every season has its scents – spring the fresh fragrance of hyacinths (*Hyacinthus orientalis*) and daffodils (*Narcissus* cvs.), both ideal for containers, and the sweet scent of wisteria, *Clematis montana* and lilacs (*Syringa* cvs.), which mingle with the light, summer scents of roses and pinks (*Dianthus* spp.).

These make way for the heady perfume of lilies (*Lilium auratum* and *L. regale* can be container-grown), and *Buddleia* spp. The exotic scents of jasmine (*Jasminum officinale*), gladioli (*Gladiolus* cvs.) and tobacco (*Nicotiana alata*) overlap with these and last into autumn. During spring we rely on the blossoms of shrubs, such as sweet box (*Sarcococca humilis*) and *Daphne odora*, and the aromatic leaves of evergreen herbs such as rosemary (*Rosmarinus officinalis*).

Summer fragrance
Scent can be enjoyed in the smallest of spaces – here yellow roses planted alongside a seat bring a breath of sweet, summer fragrance to a gently sunlit corner.

DAPHNE
Daphne retusa

In late spring *Daphne retusa*, like many other members of the daphne genus, bears an abundance of wonderfully perfumed flowers. It has glossy, evergreen foliage, and bright, autumn berries – a worthwhile addition to any small garden.

ROSEMARY
Rosmarinus officinalis

Rosemary, of which there are many forms, has heavily aromatic, evergreen foliage which can be used to flavor food. For the full benefit of its year-round scent grow near a bench, under a window, or in a container near the kitchen door – handy for snippings to put in your cooking pot.

BROMPTON STOCK
Matthiola incana

Brompton stock has a heavy, luscious scent when in flower in mid-summer. Plant in a pot near a window or door so you can enjoy the fragrance on a warm summer's evening or use as a colorful, scented filler in a small bedding scheme.

VIBURNUM
Viburnum × carlcephalum

The spring flowers of *Viburnum × carlcephalum* are sweetly scented; it also has brilliantly-colored autumn foliage, and berries.

MOROCCAN BROOM
Cytisus battandieri

In high summer the flowers of Moroccan broom exude a sweet, pineapple-like scent. It has a spreading habit, but can be trained against a wall.

GROUND COVER PLANTING

Ground covering plants answer the call of awkward-shaped or "left-over" spaces (common in small, urban garden areas) which are difficult or even impossible to pave, or plant in a regular manner. They make an attractive, practical alternative to small areas of grass (which tend to look scruffy for much of the year and require a good deal of maintenance) and, providing the soil is cleared thoroughly before planting, make excellent weed suppressors.

Ground cover plants can be used to link taller growing plant groups within a small, mixed planting scheme, or on their own as a contrast to hard surfaces or areas of gravel. If you wish to confine your ground cover planting to a particular area, do not choose such rampant or invasive plants as creeping buttercup (*Ranunculus reptans*) or the periwinkles or myrtles (*Vinca minor* and *Vinca major*).

Low-growing plants and taller, hummock-shaped plants can be used as ground cover. Amongst the former are perennials such as *Ajuga* spp. which forms a dense mat of small leaves, *Bergenia* spp. which has large, eye-catching foliage, and the furry-leaved *Stachys lanata*. For year-round ground cover choose an evergreen shrub such as the low-growing *Cotoneaster dammeri*, or consider the many evergreen choices among creeping or slow-growing forms of juniper (*Juniperus* spp. and cvs.).

Textured mat *Three different ground cover plants creep across this small area, giving a gentle rhythmic appearance that makes a pleasing contrast with the diamond-shaped paving pattern. Above the foreground* Ajuga reptans 'Burgundy Glow' *grows the bronzy-green* Acaena microphylla *and* Geranium endressii, *a white-flowered form of crane's-bill geranium.*

GREATER PERIWINKLE
Vinca major 'Variegata'

Both *V. major* and *V. minor* make good year-round ground cover for shady spaces (though *V. major* is not reliably winter-hardy in most northern regions). They should only be used to cover spaces of a reasonable size, for they grow extremely fast.

EUONYMUS
Euonymus fortunei

The bright, evergreen foliage of *E.f.* 'Emerald 'n' Gold' gives a cheerful appearance all year round. Like the cultivar 'Silver Queen' it has a low, hummocky form of growth and makes good "shapely" ground cover. Both varieties are suited to town gardens as they are resistent to air pollution.

BUGLE
Ajuga reptans 'Atropurpurea'

The growth of this low-growing, shade-loving perennial can easily be kept under control. In spring it is studded with blue flowers which look stunning against its lustrous, purple-bronze leaves. It combines effectively with shade-loving primulas (*Primula* spp.).

SPOTTED DEAD NETTLE
Lamium maculatum 'Beacon Silver'

Despite its unattractive common name, 'Beacon Silver' is one of my ground cover favorites. It has heart-shaped, silvery leaves which brighten shady corners (it will grow in sun too) and in late spring, bright-pink flowers appear. It grows fast, but does not become as invasive as its unruly relative *L. galeobdolon.*

PLANTS FOR POTS

Pots and containers really come into their own in the small-space garden for they make it possible to grow plants of any size in any location. Also, they make it easy to move them about to create different arrangements throughout the year, and to change their location on impulse.

Plant care

Just about any type of plant, ranging from small trees to vegetables and herbs, can be grown in a container provided they are given adequate root space and are well watered and fed.

Drainage holes are essential to prevent the plant roots rotting in the sour water that will collect at the bottom of a sealed container, and also because in winter any collected water might freeze, damaging the roots and, quite possibly, the container. Place a layer of porous material, such as pebbles or broken crockery, over the drainage holes (see the planting detail on p.206).

The more humus you give a plant the better (except for those which prefer poor soil), for the amount of moisture and nutrients retained will be greater. You should always give container-grown plants a good quality growing mixture. For small pots and especially large containers, consider the lightweight soilless mixes, available in most garden centers. Plants grown in exposed sites, or in hanging baskets, should be fed and watered even more regularly than those at ground level, for the soil is likely to be dehydrated by the wind. This is especially true of plants grown on balconies or in window-boxes.

Special considerations

Terracotta containers dry out quickly, so soak them well (before use) and try lining their sides with plastic to aid moisture retention. Hanging baskets should be lined with plastic or a layer of moss. Pierce the plastic to allow stale water to drain out and the plants' roots to breath.

Striking combination *The success of this informal arrangement of planted containers stems from its striking combination of gentle, relaxed plant forms (the pink-flowered* Pelargonium peltatum cv. *and silver-gray* Helichrysum microcephalum *at the rear) with strong sculptural ones (various succulents).*

LILY-FLOWERED TULIP
Tulipa whittallii

Tulip spp. and cvs. are suited to containers – their slim stems and tapered foliage never look out of place, and there is a flower shape and color to suit the style of most containers and locations. The bulbs should be planted in late autumn in well-drained soil.

TOBACCO PLANT
Nicotiana alata

The flowers of the elegant tobacco plant have a heady fragrance. Plant in containers near a door or window to appreciate their scent from outside and in. The colors of *N. alata* range from the mixed pinks shown here, to white and green.

IMPATIENS
Impatiens walleriana

Impatiens flower from spring to autumn and are perfect for planting in containers to add seasonal color to an evergreen planting scheme, or to brighten up a doorstep or windowsill. The flower colors of impatiens include pink, white and red; this cultivar has particularly handsome foliage.

KINGFISHER DAISY
Felicia bergeriana

This small daisy is especially suitable for planting in containers in exposed locations such as roofs, balconies and windowsills, for it happily flourishes in both full sun and wind. Its dainty blue and yellow-centered flowers look attractive with the soft gold leaves of *Helichrysum* sp.

HOUSELEEK
Sempervivum tectorum

The houseleek, most commonly found in rockeries, looks extremely effective when planted in simply-shaped containers, for these will show off the satisfying texture and pattern of its fleshy rosettes to the best advantage. Happiest in full sun, and able to thrive in poor soil, they make ideal balcony plants.

PLANT AND POT STYLE

When choosing plants and pots for your garden space, bear in mind the concept of "harmony", for it is important that there is harmony of shape, size and color between the plant, the container and the surroundings, be they natural or man-made.

Proportion and color

Consider first the proportion of plant (or plants) to pot. A small, patterned pot, for example, would be dominated by a bold planting of *Phormium* sp., would look too fussy with *Lobelia* sp., but would be perfectly balanced by a simple planting of *Helichrysum* sp. Then think about the color of the plant in relation to the pot. Do you want to make a dramatic contrast or a subtle combination?

There are several styles of planting. An informal, mixed group of plants has a relaxed, charmingly muddled look, which suits older-style buildings. Sharp, modern surroundings on the other hand are usually better complemented by strong schemes of maybe just one or two striking, linear plants such as *Clivia* spp. and *Cordyline* spp.

You can vary the arrangment of pots too. With informal arrangements, the combination of plants within them should be formal enough to avoid the overall effect being messy. With formal arrangements of containers, either side of a door for instance, symmetrical planting looks striking.

When planting hanging baskets, or containers positioned high on a wall, choose plants that are effective when looked at from below or from the side. Most suitable are those whose stems and leaves meander gracefully (such as many herbs) or arch elegantly (such as Boston fern).

Subtle contrast
Purple *Berberis* 'Red Pillar' makes a subtle tonal contrast with a red terracotta container.

Herb mix This terracotta pot, planted with flowering chives, a mixture of shrubby thymes and winter savory, would make a decorative and useful terrace feature – the herbs could be replaced with crocuses for early spring color.

Swirling scheme A reconstituted stone pot in the form of a Corinthian capital makes a good textural composition with a planting of gold *Helichrysum* sp.

Scented climber
Trachelospermum jasminoides, a twining evergreen climber, has been trained into an arresting conical shape. It is a fragrant plant with charming, jasmine-like clusters of flowers.

Dramatic form
Positioning strong, contrasting forms together can have a dramatic effect, as shown here by a *Cordyline* sp. in a classical urn.

Felicia amelloides
(left) This half-hardy perennial has blue daisy-flowers over variegated foliage.

PLANTS FOR SHADE

Many small garden spaces are overshadowed by tall buildings, boundary walls, or overhanging trees. Some are cast in complete shade all the time, others get a short spell of sun as it describes its arc, before lapsing into shade again; many are just shady in parts. The range of plants that will flourish in small, shady spaces (both damp and dry) is much wider than many people suspect, for often the very structures that cast the shade also give shelter. (A list of those which prefer dry shade and those which prefer damp shade is on pp.208–9.)

Shade-loving plants often have large leaves (to enable them to photosynthesize); their flowers tend to be muted in color, and in a confined space fragrance will hang heavy on the air. Areas of shaded planting can be highly atmospheric – lush foliage around a shaded water feature perhaps, or pale flowers peeping out from a dark corner.

Shade-plant selection

Evergreen shrubs are invaluable shade "fillers". Shady urban spaces that are sheltered, in moderate winter regions, and fairly moist, are perfect for camellias. Their smooth, gleaming foliage will give shady areas an attractive luster all year round and their cup-shaded flowers a vivid splash of seasonal color.

Small and shady *The profusion of foliage in this small, shady area creates a lush, tropical effect. Large leaf shapes predominate: among the boldest are those of* Trachycarpus fortunei, *right of the small chair.*

Among my favorite perennials are the strongly-shaped *Bergenia cordifolia*, which has large leathery leaves, and *Iris foetidissima* and *Liriope muscari* which I like for their spiky, evergreen foliage. Bamboos (*Arundinaria* spp.) will grow in any dry, sheltered, and shady spot. Their tall, vertical forms make an interesting contrast with the fronded, curved foliage of ferns. For a more delicate touch, plant Japanese anemones (*Anemone × hybrida*) which have dainty flowers and spreading growth. Lilies (*Lilium* spp. and cvs.) will grow in pots; they have exotic flower forms and many kinds will scent your shaded retreat.

If your shaded area is always moist, under the drip of an established tree for instance, plant the large-leaved *Rheum palmatum* and *Gunnera manicata* for an exotic, "tropical rain forest" effect. Other suitable shrubs for moist areas include hydrangeas, and *Viburnum davidii* and *V. rhytidophyllum*. Plants of the genus *Hosta* need plenty of moisture and are great shade survivors (if you can keep the snails, which are so fond of them, at bay).

SOFT SHIELD FERN
Polystichum setiferum

Ferns are indispensable shade-lovers – their fronded foliage and arching form bring atmospheric interest to all manner of awkwardly-shaped nooks and crannies. Most useful are those which are evergreen, like *Polystichum setiferum*.

JAPANESE LAUREL
Aucuba japonica 'Salicifolia'

The gleaming green leaves and bright-red berries of this form of *Aucuba japonica* will bring a breath of life to the driest and shadiest of corners (variegated forms such as *Aucuba japonica* 'Variegata' thrive better in light shade). Being tolerant of atmospheric pollution it is ideally suited to town and city gardens.

WINDFLOWER
Anemone × hybrida 'Honorine Jobert'

Anemone × hybrida is one of my personal favorites, for it has a simple flower shape, tall, elegant stems, handsome foliage, and will grow in light shade. It is long-lived, but resents disturbance once it has become properly established.

LILY-OF-THE-VALLEY
Convallaria majalis

Lily-of-the-valley, a lover of moist shady conditions, fills the spring air with an exquisite fragrance. The foliage is simple and neat; the flowers dainty.

SPURGE
Euphorbia robbiae

Euphorbia robbiae grows well in dry shade, its rosettes of leaves forming a textured, evergreen mat which is covered by yellow flowers in spring.

BERGENIA
Bergenia 'Abendglut'

In mid-to-late winter thick flower stems start to rise from the huge, leathery foliage of *Bergenia* 'Abendglut'; by spring they are covered with pink bell-shaped blooms. Its foliage makes excellent shade ground cover.

OREGON GRAPE
Mahonia aquifolium

This small, tough, evergreen shrub has bright-yellow spring flowers and blue-black autumn berries, and makes good ground cover in dry, shady sites. It is resilient enough to grow in exposed sites, such as balconies.

LILY TURF
Liriope muscari

Liriope muscari can be grown in containers and can thus be enjoyed in the smallest of shady sites; it also makes excellent ground cover. By early autumn the tall stems that rise from the elegant leaves are covered with tiny droplet-shaped flowers.

HYDRANGEA
Hydrangea macrophylla serrata

The pale mauve blossoms of the Lacecap cultivar 'Bluebird' gleam against its shaded foliage, right. Hydrangeas are excellent "urban-dwellers", for they can be grown in containers, are unaffected by atmospheric pollution, and thrive in sheltered, lightly-shaded sites. They do however, need moisture.

The blooms of Lacecap hydrangeas, like those of the Mophead forms, grow blue in acid soil and grow pink in alkaline soil

CORSICAN HELLEBORE
Helleborus lividus corsicus

The gray-green foliage and pale green flowers of this evergreen perennial bring immense cheer to shady corners during the dull days of late winter and early spring. It looks effective against a dark-leaved evergreen such as *Aucuba japonica*.

PLANTS FOR EXPOSED SITES

Plants on roofs, balconies and high window-ledges are exposed to far greater extremes of heat, cold and wind than those at ground level. The wind not only buffets plants, but dehydrates the soil in which they are grown, an effect intensified by the sun. However, there is a considerable range of plants that are able to survive such inhospitable conditions (a list is given on pp.209–10), and many others that can survive a season, or longer if shelter is provided by a fence, canvas windbreak or tough shrub, such as a form of common juniper.

Plants grown in containers (as those grown above ground level are likely to be) have a limited nutrient and moisture reserve so always use a nutrient-rich, moisture-retentive medium and water frequently.

Tough permanent planting
Tough shrubby material can be used to give year-round interest, and to shelter yourself and less hardy plants from the wind. Look to those which are adapted to survive conditions on open ground such as on fields, mountainsides, or by the sea. All the broom family are tough (*Cytisus* spp., *Genista* spp. and *Spartium* spp.), as are the gorse family (*Ulex* spp.), some heaths and heathers and evergreen

Roof-top planting *A stout wooden framework, infilled with bamboo matting, screens this roof-top from the wind, allowing plants with flamboyant architectural form, such as* Fatsia japonica *(by the screen) and* Euphorbia wulfenii *(foreground), to survive.*

and "evergray" herbs, most conifers and many grasses. Climbers in exposed locations are likely to take a considerable beating from the wind, so stick to deciduous ones (these are naturally tougher than evergreens) such as Virginia creeper (*Parthenocissus quinquefolia*) and honeysuckle (*Lonicera* spp.). Alternatively use resilient evergreen climbers like ivy (*Hedera* spp.).

Plants for seasonal interest
Many plants will survive a season on a balcony, window-ledge, or roof-top, particularly if they can be given shelter and are well looked after. Mass spring and summer bulbs and annuals in containers to add a flamboyant dash of seasonal color. Plants with a daisy flower are usually tough; these range from the smallest blue daisy (*Felicia* spp.), through to the exuberant yellow *Rudbeckia* forms and a long-standing favorite, white *Chrysanthemum* × *superbum*.

SEA BUCKTHORN
Hippophae rhamnoides

The coast is the natural habitat of this vigorous gray shrub, making it ideal for windswept balconies and roofs. If a male shrub is planted windward of a female, red berries will result. With age, buckthorn becomes a statuesque small tree.

HOUSELEEK
Sempervivum hirtum

This rock plant grows best in poor, fast-draining soil, so add grit to the soil mixture. It looks effective grown *en masse* in a shallow container. There are many species of *Sempervivum*, varying in size from the tiniest rosette to the size of a saucer.

VIBURNUM
Viburnum betulifolium

V. betulifolium is well suited to exposed areas and grows well in soil with good drainage. This is an erect form, bearing white flowers in early summer. To ensure a profusion of red berries in the autumn, two or more shrubs must be planted together.

BROOM
Cytisus nigricans

A species of *Cytisus*, unusual in that its long, spiky yellow flowers appear throughout late summer; the other genus members flower in late spring. They are all hardy plants, able to thrive in poor soil and survive strong winds and are therefore ideal for high window-boxes or balconies. Cut back after plants have finished flowering.

COTTON LAVENDER
Santolina pinnata

A hardy evergreen shrub that thrives in full sun, dry soils and withstands strong winds – the perfect roof and balcony plant. It has fully divided green leaves and tiny cream flowers. They can be grown in troughs as a low hedge (plant about 23cm (9 in) apart).

COUNTRY-STYLE PLANTING

Most people have an image of the country garden – of its full, billowing outlines, gentle colors, soft fragrances and air of calm – and many yearn to capture these characteristics in their small garden-space, among apartment blocks and busy roads, and the general hurly-burly of urban life.

There are many plants which evoke the country garden "feel"; some of my favorites are shown on the following three pages. Such plants can be combined to create a tapestry of country planting in a small bedding scheme, or just one or two, planted in containers, used to give your doorstep, windowsill or balcony a country look.

Creating a country tapestry

Though at first glance the true country garden appears to be the result of relaxed, almost random planting, beneath the "flesh" lie "bones", in the form of paths, walls, arches and other hard elements, and bold, structural planting, which prevent the informal planting scheme becoming a jumbled mess. Even in a small, town space, any bedding scheme of essentially non-architectural country planting, such as love-in-a-mist (*Nigella damascena*), lupines (*Lupinus* cvs.), and delphinium (*Delphinium* cvs.), needs to be punctuated by permanent features such as a bench, a piece of sculpture and/or plants with bold form,

Country composition *There is a calm harmony of color among the greens, grays and yellows of this small, country planting scheme. A stone trough, wooden bench and tall hollyhock give structure to the informal arrangement which includes gold* Alchemilla mollis *and silver* Santolina chamaecyparissus *(far right) and cream* Sisyrinchium sp. *(left).*

like the evergreen shrubs Mexican orange (*Choisya ternata*), rosemary (*Rosmarinus officinalis*), and sage (*Salvia officinalis*). These will calm and steady your country tapestry when annuals and perennials burst into flower and give it shape and interest during the winter months.

One of the charms of the country garden is its fullness, which comes from plants smothering walls and bursting out of their beds. This look can be created in the smallest of spaces by allowing self-seeders to grow through gravel and between the cracks in paving, and by covering walls and fences with climbing plants.

Do not be tempted to give your urban "country garden" a sentimental overlay of "olde-worlde" charm with "yesteryear" artefacts, for this will immediately give it a contrived and self-conscious appearance – rely instead on the colors, scents, and textures of your "country" plants and the style of indigenous features.

LADY'S MANTLE
Alchemilla mollis

Lady's mantle grows in sun or shade and, when covered with swathes of bright-green flower heads, will instantly give the smallest of urban spaces a relaxed country atmosphere. After a fall of rain its leaves retain pearly droplets of water.

RUBUS
Rubus 'Benenden'

This medium-sized deciduous shrub, which grows to a height of 3m (10 ft), has a grace and charm which typifies the country-garden look; its loose, relaxed form is not unlike that of the shrub rose. In late spring/early summer single, eye-catching white flowers appear along its slender branches.

ANGELICA
Angelica archangelica

The huge, green heads of this summer-flowering herb are balanced by lush, aromatic foliage, making it a perfect way of bringing a breath of country air to a small, town space. Plant alongside *Foeniculum vulgare* which flowers into mid-autumn.

SNAKE'S HEAD
Fritillaria meleagris

Fritillaria meleagris has a gentle appeal. It may take two or three seasons to establish, but your patience will be amply rewarded by pendulous flowers in spring.

SHASTA DAISY
Chrysanthemum × *superbum*

Shasta daisies have a simple, refreshing appearance redolent of the cottage garden. They flower for approximately two months during the summer.

179

CALIFORNIA POPPY
Eschscholzia californica

MULLEIN
Verbascum 'Gainsborough'

One way of creating a soft, country look in town is to allow self-seeders to establish themselves in gravel.

Here, orange California poppies make a delicate and informal composition – a possibility for the smallest of gravelled spaces.

The spire-like stems of *Verbascum* 'Gainsborough' grow to a height of 1.2m (4 ft) and bear apricot-yellow flowers throughout the summer. Plant alongside the spring-flowering bulbs *Narcissus poeticus*, to create a seasonally-changing tapestry.

LILAC
Syringa villosa

LOVE-IN-A-MIST
Nigella damascena

SHRUB ROSE
Rosa 'Constance Spry'

Flopping over a white bench seat the voluptuous *Rosa* 'Constance Spry' typifies high summer in a country setting. This successor to the old-fashioned cabbage rose will bring a refreshing and fragrant breath of air to the smallest of urban spaces, for it is equally happy growing as a spreading bush as clambering up a wall. Though it only flowers once a year, in early summer, the spectacular effect is certainly worth waiting for.

The sight and scent of spring lilac blossoms are an evocation of the shapes and fragrances of summer not far behind. Plant in well-drained soil in a sunny site.

The delicate flowers and fine foliage of 'Persian Jewel' combine here to create a soft, hazy effect. Grow in full sun in well-drained soil.

ARCHITECTURAL PLANTING

Architectural plants are the horticultural equivalent of exclamation marks and dramatic pauses. They have a strong overall form which comes from dramatic leaf, stem, or branch shape and can be used in isolation to make a single bold statement, or to give structural backbone to a mixed scheme of loosely-formed planting.

The effect of architectural plants varies, according to their shape. The Italian cyprus (*Cupressus sempervirens* 'Stricta') has a slim, elegant form that makes an eye-catching outline against urban landscapes and open skylines: Irish yew (*Taxus baccata* 'Fastigiata') does the same in a more robust way. At the shrubby level, architectural plants include *Fatsia japonica* and × *Fatshedera lizei*. Both can be grown in containers and have flamboyant foliage that particularly suits urban locations. For a pleasing rounded outline choose *Choisya ternata*, and for a spiky silhouette, yuccas and phormiums.

Perennials with architectural merit include the genus *Hosta* and *Bergenia cordifolia* cultivars. Planted in bold masses they will punctuate and steady the fuzzy accumulation of other perennials, whose fleeting merit is their flower. Climbers with strong leaf shape, such as the rather vigorous, wine-producing grape vine (*Vitis coignetiae*), and all the large-leafed *Hedera* genus, are in an excellent way of bringing shape and pattern to all manner of vertical surfaces. For a full list of plants with architectural merit see pages 213–4.

Architectural contrast
Among "softer" plants, the robust spiked form of agave is the horticultural equivalent of an exclamation mark. En masse the agaves' strong sculptural forms complement the craggy outlines of stone buildings as in the Mediterranean garden shown here.

STAG'S HORN SUMAC
Rhus typhina 'Laciniata'

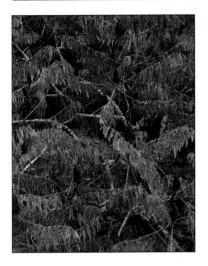

The cut-leaf stag's horn sumac has a good craggy form. The antler-shaped branches are emphasized after leaf fall.

EUPHORBIA
Euphorbia wulfenii

The species *Euphorbia wulfenii* has a strong, but relaxed form of growth. 'Lambrook Gold' has brilliant flowers.

RODGERSIA
Rodgersia podophylla

This perennial has enormous leaves, up to 30cm (1 ft) in width, and spires of creamy flowers. It grows well in moist conditions and makes a good contrast with water plants with a vertical form, such as *Iris laevigata* (shown on p.185).

MEXICAN ORANGE
Choisya ternata

This evergreen shrub has a gently rounded form that will give your garden space a pleasing, gentle rhythm all year round if you live in mild-winter regions. In late spring its glossy, green foliage is offset by large clusters of fragrant white flowers. It can be planted in sun or light shade.

CABBAGE TREE
Cordyline australis

C. australis has a strongly vertical form and long sword-shaped leaves, which look striking against a plain backdrop. Not for cold winter areas.

GIANT HOGWEED
Heracleum mantegazzianum

This invasive self-seeding perennial has large umbrella-shaped flower heads and flamboyant foliage. Introduced individually in a small space the effect is dramatic. The dead seed heads must be removed before they drop to prevent it spreading.

ALLIUM
Allium rosenbachianum

Spherical heads of tightly compacted mauve-pink flowers appear in early summer making this a plant for seasonal architectural interest. It reaches a height of 76cm (30 in) and looks effective rising through a plant such as *Mesembryanthemum criniflorum*, which has a low spreading habit.

PLANTAIN LILY
Hosta spp. and cvs.

No list of architectural plants should be without hostas. They all have a strong overall pattern of ribbed, textured leaves which will bring sculptural strength to the smallest and shadiest of spaces. *Hosta sieboldiana elegans*, top, has larger, darker leaves than its variegated relation *Hosta fortunei* 'Albapicta', above.

ORNAMENTAL RHUBARB
Rheum palmatum

JAPANESE WATER IRIS
Iris laevigata

The architectural strength of the Japanese water iris lies in the shape of its vertical leaves which form a spiky mass and make a striking backdrop to the rich purple flowers that appear in early summer. It grows best in shallow water or very moist soil.

BLUE-EYED GRASS
Sisyrinchium striatum

Huge eye-catching leaves up to 1m (3 ft) in width and foaming spires of rust-colored flowers up to 2m (6 ft) high (appearing in mid-summer) give this perennial an energetic outline. For maximum effect grow it in isolation from other plants. Its leaves tend to wilt in the sun so plant in a moist, shady area.

En masse the elegant lanceolate leaves and dainty, cream flowers of blue-eyed grass make a refreshing contrast with a shrub of spreading habit like the *Elaeagnus pungens* shown here, or a simple backdrop such as a painted wall. This perennial self-seeder will grow in just about any soil, but prefers sun.

TOPIARY

Though topiary (the art of clipping plants to shape) brings to the mind's eye images of seventeenth-century country gardens, decorated with grand pyramids of yew and peacocks of box, in a scaled-down form it is just as relevant to small, urban spaces today. Topiary's neatly-tailored shapes suit the strong lines and hard shapes of man-made environments.

Topiary styles

Plants cut into contrasted shapes (see pp.188–9 for techniques) can be grouped together to make a dramatic display against a plain backdrop such as a painted wall, or single plants used as individual points of emphasis in the overall design of a space. Simple, geometric shapes suit small spaces better than complex, figurative ones. Where topiary plants are adjacent to a building why not echo the shape of architectural features (even a window shape) in your clipping? In early twentieth-century Scandinavian gardens, hedging plants were neatly clipped to give strong, linear definition which contrasted with the natural, loose shapes of other plants. Following this tradition, but in small space, you might clip a hedging plant such as box to create a simple pattern, and contrast it with a plain background such as a pale-coloured gravel, or softer plant forms. Topiary plants always look most effective in simple containers (ornate ones will distract) and can be used to bring a theatrical flavor to the smallest of spaces, such as a doorstep or narrow passageway.

Plant care

Many topiary plants are naturally greedy feeders, and their demands increase as they are clipped back and attempt to put out new shoots, so always use a rich soil, and feed and water them regularly. Place them in sunlight to encourage maximum growth and keep out of strong winds.

Formal versatility (above and right) *Small-leaved evergreens, tightly-clipped into formal shapes, suit both schemes that continue the formal theme, as in the composition including stone sculpture, above, and those that are more relaxed, opposite, where they contrast with loose and natural forms.*

SHAPING PLANTS

The plants most suitable for topiary have a slow and dense growth, and are able to withstand frequent clipping. Of the evergreens there is box (*Buxus sempervirens*), holly (*Ilex* spp.) and yew (*Taxus baccata*), and of the deciduous plants, beech (*Fagus* spp.), hawthorn (*Crataegus* spp.) and some privets (*Ligustrum* spp.). A small range of conifers, including Lawson cypress (*Chamaecyparis lawsoniana*) and Leyland cypress (*Cupressocyparis leylandii*) can be clipped too. Some plants of loose habit, such as fuchsias, *Olearia* spp. and *Hibiscus* spp., can also be pruned to shape. (See p.216 for a full list.)

Clip young plants of dense growth three to four times a year; mature plants should need clipping once or twice a year. Complex shapes can be created by placing chicken-wire of the desired shape over the young plant and clipping back the new growth as it protrudes through the wire.

Plants of looser growth like the *Olearia* sp. and *Fuchsia* hybrid below, can be pruned to bush out at the top above a bare stem. Clip or pinch the leader branch to encourage side shooting and remove all shoots from the bottom of the stem (see p.205).

Spherical box
Buxus sempervirens clipped into a sphere can be used as a contrast amongst pots of annuals.

Standard fuchsia
Fuchsia 'Mission Bells' is a seasonal topiary feature, for it is of most interest when in flower and it has an elegant and delicate style.

Whimsical feature (right) *Privet and* Helichrysum *sp. have been combined to create a whimsical topiary basket, grown in a simple container. The dark green of the privet, which has been trained and clipped around a wire shape, contrasts with the loose form of pale silver* Helichrysum *sp.*

Summer feature
A *Chrysanthemum frutescens* clipped into shape.

Shaped hibiscus
The trimmed stem of *Hibiscus syriacus* emphasizes the shape of its vertical branches.

Conical box
Buxus sempervirens makes a tailored contrast with the *Chrysanthemum* sp. behind it.

PLANTS FOR WATER

The smallest and most formal of water features can be enhanced by planting both in the water and around it. Recreating the natural pond look (both in the style of water feature and planting) in a small-space garden is not to be recommended, for this leads to a contrived and self-conscious appearance. (Construction details for a variety of formal water features are shown on p.201.)

Planting in water

The smaller the area of water the more restrained both the number and variety of plants should be. A strong effect can be created by simply planting one type of plant in a pool, or if you have a collection of water-filled barrels, a different type of water plant in each. The vertical stems and leaves of irises, sedges and flags can be used as a dramatic contrast to the smooth surface of still water. Plants with floating leaves have a more restful appearance. If space allows, a combination of horizontal and vertical plant forms can be used. Marginal plants with vertical or arching forms make an effective visual counterbalance to a water jet or water pouring from a spout.

Floating aquatics such as water lilies should be planted in plant baskets or pots. Marginal plants (which grow in shallow water) should be similarly planted and placed on a step at a suitable height in the water (see p.207 for planting details).

Planting around water

Plants can be used to soften the division between a formal water feature and the rest of the garden, to extend the mood of any planting in a pool and to make reflections in the water. Plants with lush foliage such as hostas, ferns and bamboos are moisture-loving and naturally suit a waterside setting. If the area around your water feature is not naturally damp, grow them in containers, and water plentifully.

Plants and water
The formal lines of this small pool have been softened by planting in the water and around it. The smooth horizontal surface of the water is contrasted by the vertical forms of sweet flags (Acorus calamus 'Variegatus') *and arum lilies* (Zantedeschia aethiopica) *that rise from it. The lush green foliage around the pool and cool flower colors create a languid atmosphere.*

BOG ARUM
Lysichiton americanum

This handsome waterside plant has rich yellow flowers that appear in early spring. Its large, smooth leaves follow and grow to a height of 1.2m (4 ft). Its size and dramatic appearance make it a plant to be used individually, rather than with others.

PLANTAIN LILY
Hosta lancifolia

Plant hostas in damp soil to create a luxuriant surround to a lightly-shaded water feature. *H. lancifolia* has smaller, more elegant leaves than many others within the genus. Its deep lilac blooms appear towards the end of summer, when few other waterside plants or aquatics are in flower, and last into autumn.

WATER LILY
Nymphaea 'Virginalis'

The pure white, tapered petals of *N.* 'Virginalis' make a cool contrast with its dark green foliage. Though it is slow to establish, patience pays off, for it has one of the longest flowering seasons of any water lily, often more than four months.

WATER POPPY
Hydrocleys nymphoides

For a refreshing composition plant the yellow-flowered water poppy in a wooden tub (filled three-quarters full of soil and a quarter full of water).

SWEET FLAG
Acorus calamus 'Variegatus'

The spiky vertical form of this rush makes a clean contrast with the smooth, horizontal surface of still water. It is a marginal plant and grows in shallow water.

GIANT MARSH MARIGOLD
Caltha polypetala

Larger than the more commonly seen *C. palustris* (marsh marigold), *C. polypetala* has saucer-shaped leaves, and multi-branched stems of clear yellow flowers which last from spring into early summer. Plant in damp soil or shallow water.

WATER PLANTAIN
Alisma plantago-aquatica

The long stalks of this shallow-water plant hold its clumps of pointed green leaves well above the water line. Delicate flower stalks (which rise to a height of 60cm (2 ft) and a mass of tiny, white flowers create a hazy summer background to the stronger shapes of the plantain-like leaves.

WATER LILY
Nymphaea 'Escarboucle'

The strident coloring of this water lily (deep-red petals with deep-yellow anthers, and dark-green leaves) make it one that is best appreciated on its own, rather than in association with other aquatics. Plant in a medium-sized rather than small pool, for a single plant will spread to a width of approximately 2m (6 ft). It will grow in water up to 45cm (1½ ft) deep and once established will bear an abundance of blooms which last from summer through to early autumn.

CONSTRUCTION & PLANTING DETAILS

This series of detailed illustrations and
practical tips covers aspects of construction
ranging from the design of a pergola to
making a water feature, and planting details
ranging from how to plant in gravel to
making topiary shapes.

CONSTRUCTION DETAILS

The construction details on these pages will be useful to you whether you are designing or building a structure yourself or obtaining estimates and briefing someone to do it for you. They show not only how to make a structure safe and practical but how to style it to suit your space.

In a small area good use can be made of space by constructing features so they have a dual function. A low retaining wall, for instance, can be constructed so it is a suitable height for an area of planting and can also be used as low-level seating; or a pergola, designed primarily to give permanent definition to an area of paving, can be fitted to support an occasional awning for shade from the sun during summer.

To give your small plot the unified look that will make it appear larger, the design and materials of any new structure, be it a water feature or flight of steps, should bear a close relationship (both in the materials used and its design) to the exterior of your home and any structures already existing in your garden space.

Before building a new structure check local bylaws and planning regulations, particularly if it is to be somewhere highly visible such as a rooftop. If you have *any* doubts as to the safety of a structure, for instance the strength of a wall or the weight a balcony can support, seek specialist advice, for if a structure collapses the ensuing calamity will be your responsibility.

WALLING

Brick walls
Engineering and facing bricks are the most suitable for exterior use. Common bricks can be used too, but they need to be rendered or plastered because they have no finish and are subject to weathering. All types of wall need strong foundations; the depth of these depend on the height of the wall, its intended function, the nature of the soil and the depth to which frost will penetrate.

Blockwork walls
Concrete blocks are cheaper than brick and come in various dimensions. When using them to build a retaining wall, steel reinforcing rods should be inserted and the block hollows strengthened by being filled with concrete.

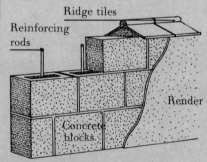

Single-width blockwork wall
Concrete blocks can be painted.

Copings
Copings (or cappings) are needed to stop rainwater seeping into the top of a wall. You can use wall bricks themselves as a coping, or a contrasting material.

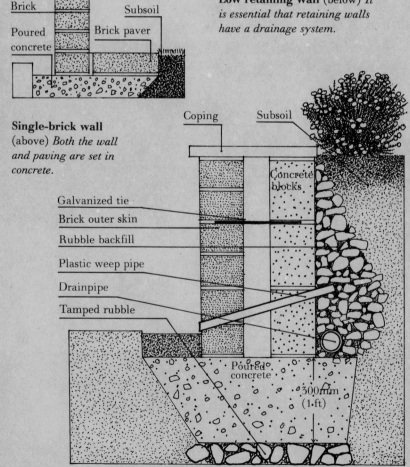

Single-brick wall (above) *Both the wall and paving are set in concrete.*

Low retaining wall (below) *It is essential that retaining walls have a drainage system.*

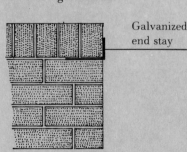

Brick-on-edge coping *Engineering bricks are the most suitable.*

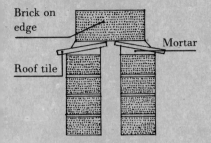

Tile and brick coping *Tiles under bricks give added protection.*

Precast swimming pool edging *This edging can be used as a seat.*

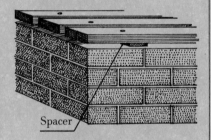

Wooden seating on a brick bench *The wood is raised to prevent rot.*

FENCING AND PLANT SUPPORTS

Trellis and wire

Trellis can be used to make free-standing screens, or used to decorate a flat surface – in both roles it can function as a plant support. Wires stretched between supports make a lightweight form of fence/plant support.

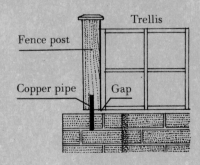

Trelliswork extension *Raise the trellis to prevent it from rotting.*

Hinged trellis *Panels of trelliswork can be hinged at the bottom to make it easy to lower them for maintenance.*

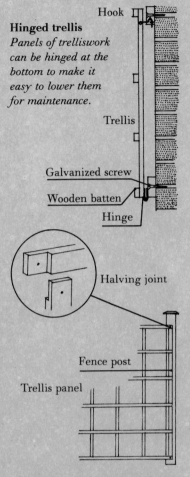

Trelliswork screen *Nail trellis to fence posts to make a screen.*

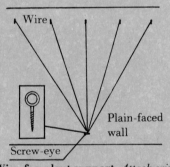

Wire-fan plant support *Attach wire using galvanized screw eyes.*

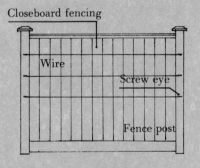

Stretched wire plant support *Stretch wire between fence posts.*

Post fixings

Because lumber rots in direct contact with the ground, wooden fence posts should be protected by one of the three methods which are illustrated below and firmly anchored in the ground.

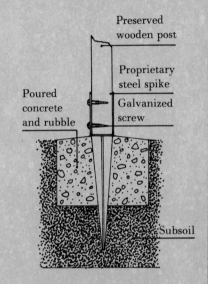

Metal spike *A wooden post and a proprietary metal spike.*

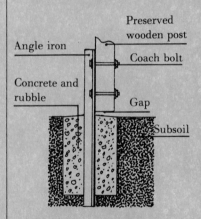

Drilled angle-iron *A wooden post and a drilled angle-iron.*

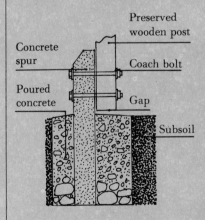

Concrete spur *A wooden post attached to a concrete spur.*

Panel fencing

Hardwood is the most long-lasting type of wood for fencing, followed by seasoned softwood treated with a preservative (under pressure so the wood becomes thoroughly impregnated).

Marine plywood fences

(right) *Treated marine plywood cut into shapes and glued to a marine plywood panel to make an abstract pattern.*

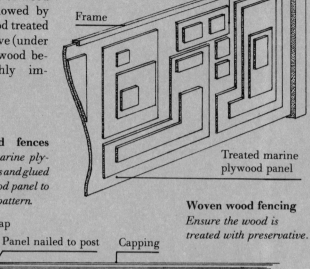

Marine plywood shapes

Frame

Treated marine plywood panel

Woven wood fencing
Ensure the wood is treated with preservative.

Fence post cap

Panel nailed to post   Capping

Closeboard fencing

Like all wooden fencing, treat regularly with a preservative.

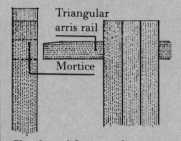

Triangular arris rail

Mortice

Closeboard fence and post

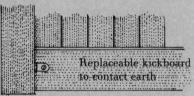

Replaceable kickboard to contact earth

Closeboard fence and ground
Use a replaceable kickboard.

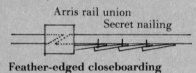

Arris rail union

Secret nailing

Feather-edged closeboarding

GATES

Types of gate

Make sure that the style, material and decorative detailing of your gate suits its surroundings and pay attention to the style of the gate's "furnishings", for instance the style of its handle or latch and the choice of hinge, all of which should suit the gate's overall style. When constructing or buying a gate remember that all types must have strong side supports (stakes) and (in the case of tall gates) cross braces to prevent the gate panels from dropping.

Plan view of tongue and groove joints

Traditional gate *Crossbraces strengthen this tall gate.*

Galvanized hinge   Crossbraces

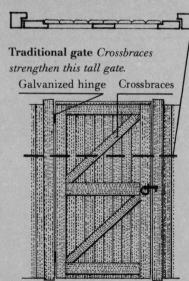

Pintle and eye hinge

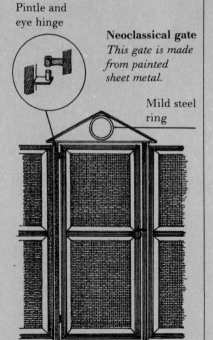

Neoclassical gate
This gate is made from painted sheet metal.

Mild steel ring

ARCHES

Styling an arch

The key to a good looking arch is the scaled relationship between the vertical and horizontal elements and the attention paid to the style of its detail.

Angular arch
This arch is supported by painted scaffolding poles.

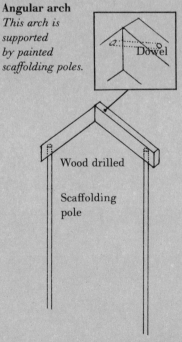

Dowel

Wood drilled

Scaffolding pole

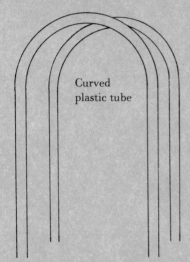

Plastic tubing arch *Colorful plastic tubing can be used to make a modern style of arch.*

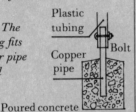

Anchorage *The plastic tubing fits over a copper pipe set in poured concrete.*

PERGOLAS

Methods of fixing

Whatever the function of your pergola (see pp.108–11) it is critical to pay attention to the style of its detailing (such as the method of fixing horizontal to vertical) as this will affect its overall look. The method of joining a free-standing pergola's horizontals to verticals will depend on the type and shape of the materials, which in turn will have been influenced by the overall look which you are seeking to achieve.

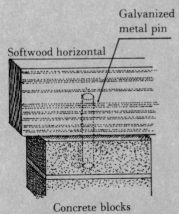

Wood to concrete *Use a galvanized metal pin.*

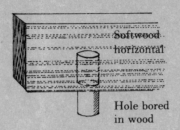

Pole to wooden crossbeam *Bore a hole in the crossbeam.*

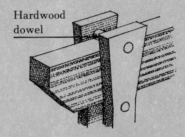

Crossbeam and forked support *Use hardwood dowels.*

Horizontal to a wall

Horizontals can be supported by two walls or by a wall at one end and free-standing pergola verticals at the other.

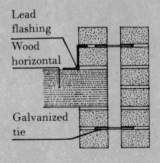

Wood into wall *The beam can be inserted into a cavity wall.*

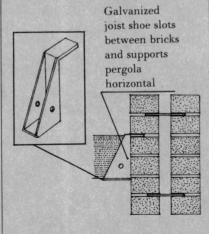

Wood into joist shoe *The beam can be supported by a joist shoe.*

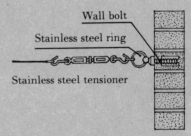

Tensioned wire to wall *Attach the tensioner to a wall bolt.*

Vertical into ground

Wooden verticals must not be in direct contact with the ground.

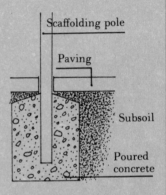

Using concrete *The vertical is anchored in poured concrete.*

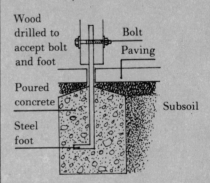

Using a steel foot *The vertical is supported by a painted steel foot.*

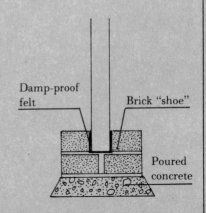

Using a brick shoe *The vertical is supported by a brick shoe.*

AWNINGS

Choosing the material

If your awning is to withstand a considerable battering from the elements use canvas lashed to a strong frame – sailcloth is ideal.

Free-standing awning (right) *A simple free-standing awning for shade can be constructed from sailcloth lashed to a tubular frame.*

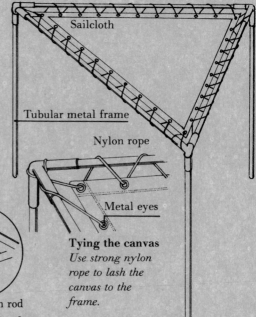

Sailcloth

Tubular metal frame

Nylon rope

Metal eyes

Tying the canvas *Use strong nylon rope to lash the canvas to the frame.*

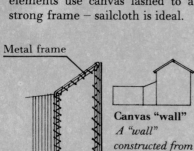

Metal frame

Canvas "wall" *A "wall" constructed from canvas lashed to a metal frame can be used to provide a small garden with privacy.*

Rope lashed to canvas and frame

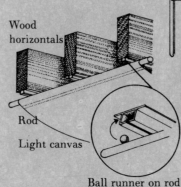

Wood horizontals

Rod

Light canvas

Ball runner on rod

Swag awning *The underside of a pergola's beams can be used to support a swag awning.*

PAVING

Special considerations

Whatever the material, style, or extent of your paving you should always create a fall for drainage into an area of planting or gravel, or a purpose-built soakaway. Where winters are cold and the subsoil is likely to freeze, paving must have extra thick foundations to prevent "lifting" or thin ones so the paving can "ride" the frost. Paving also varies according to whether it is for pedestrian or vehicular use.

25mm (1 in) sand

75mm (3 in) tamped rubble

Pedestrian use   Subsoil   Mortar

75mm (3 in) dry mix mortar bed

100mm (4 in) tamped rubble

Vehicular use   Subsoil

Large unit paving *Large, regular stone or concrete paving slabs are quicker to lay than irregularly-shaped pieces of old stone.*

Mortar brushed in as dry mix

25mm (1 in) dry mix mortar bed

75mm (3 in) tamped rubble

Pedestrian use   Subsoil

75mm (3 in) dry mix mortar bed

100mm (4 in) tamped rubble

Vehicular use   Subsoil

Small unit paving *Bricks, stone blocks, or concrete pavers are the most common small unit paving materials.*

75mm (3 in) concrete

50mm (2 in) tamped rubble

Pedestrian use   Subsoil

Mild steel reinforcing grid

100mm (4 in) poured concrete

75mm (3 in) tamped rubble

Vehicular use   Subsoil

Poured concrete paving *The aggregate can be revealed by brushing and hosing the concrete before it is completely set.*

Natural stone

75mm (3 in) mortar bed absorbs irregular shape of natural stone to provide flat surface

100mm (4 in) tamped rubble

Pedestrian use   Subsoil

Natural stone paving *Lay such paving in a bed of mortar.*

10mm ($\frac{1}{3}$ in) top dressing

Edging

25mm (1 in) gravel rolled into sand and gravel

Pedestrian use

75mm (3 in) consolidated sand and gravel

Consolidated gravel *Use an edging to divide areas of gravel.*

DECKS

Making a safe deck

Consult a joiner on joist distancing and lumber dimensions you will need for your deck. Make sure the framework that supports the deck is robust and set in strong concrete foundations. Never penny-pinch when constructing decking – the result could be dangerous.

Deck junctions

An area of deck can adjoin another area of decking, another surfacing material or a door. Ensure there is a drainage channel beneath the junctions.

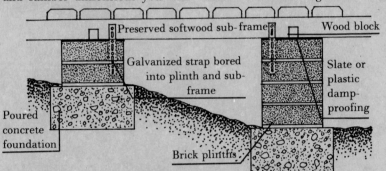

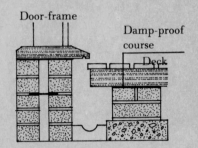

Junction between deck and door

Uneven site Decks can be used to make a flat surface over an uneven site.

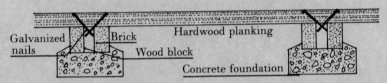

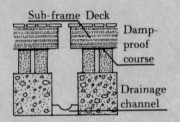

Junction between deck and deck

Even site Decks can be used as an alternative to paving.

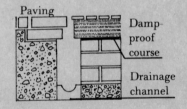

Junction between deck and paving

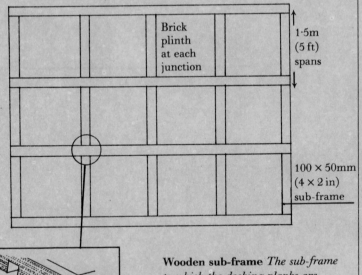

Brick plinth at each junction

1·5m (5 ft) spans

100 × 50mm (4 × 2 in) sub-frame

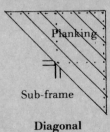

Halving joint

Wooden sub-frame *The sub-frame to which the decking planks are nailed can be constructed from hardwood or seasoned softwood. The frame should be supported by a plinth at each junction.*

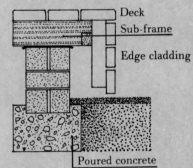

Deck
Sub-frame
Edge cladding
Poured concrete

Edge cladding *Clad the end of the deck with timber for a neat finish.*

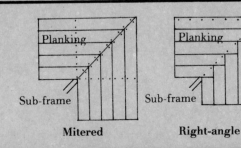

Deck patterns

Decking planks can be laid diagonally as well as horizontally. The shape of the sub-frame, picked up in the pattern of the nailing, makes a decorative touch. Try to choose a pattern that suits the style of any adjoining buildings.

Planking / Sub-frame — **Diagonal**

Planking / Sub-frame — **Mitered**

Planking / Sub-frame — **Right-angle**

STEPS

Types of steps

Step dimensions depend on the height you need to climb and the distance in which you have to do it. Flights of steps can be used to get from A to B, or just a few steps can be used as part of the garden's design, to make a change in level. Like paving, steps need drainage.

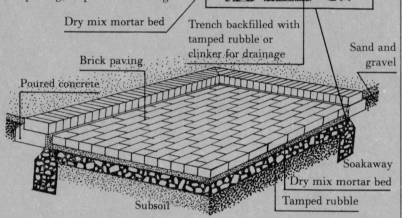

Pea shingle

Brick

Drainage slope

Dry mix mortar bed

Trench backfilled with tamped rubble or clinker for drainage

Sand and gravel

Brick paving

Poured concrete

Soakaway

Dry mix mortar bed

Tamped rubble

Subsoil

Steps between two levels *A single shallow step or several shallow steps can be used to make a gentle change in level in your garden. Ensure that a soakaway for drainage is included in the design of the steps.*

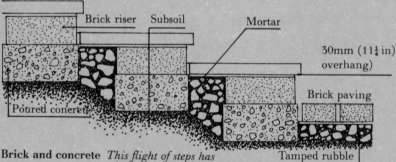

Concrete slab tread

Brick riser   Subsoil

Mortar

30mm (11¼ in) overhang)

Brick paving

Poured concrete

Tamped rubble

Brick and concrete *This flight of steps has precast concrete treads (the horizontal elements) mortared to brick risers (the vertical elements) over consolidated hardcore.*

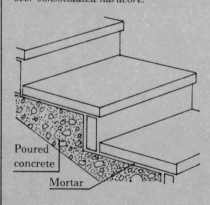

Poured concrete

Mortar

Flight of concrete steps *This flight of steps has precast concrete treads and concrete risers.*

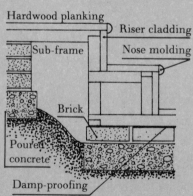

Hardwood planking

Riser cladding

Sub-frame

Nose molding

Brick

Poured concrete

Damp-proofing

Deck steps *Wooden steps with concrete foundations can be used to link two areas of deck.*

Handrails

Handrails make flights of steps, particularly steep ones, safer to use and at the same time can make an attractive decorative addition to their overall appearance. Make sure the material and shape of a handrail suits the style and material of the steps which it adjoins. A selection of designs of different styles of handrails is shown below.

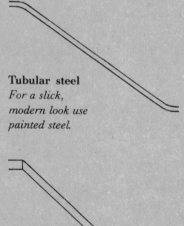

Tubular steel *For a slick, modern look use painted steel.*

Softwood *Paint or stain a softwood handrail to complement the color of your steps.*

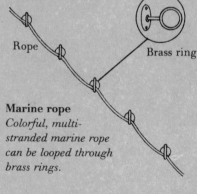

Rope

Brass ring

Marine rope *Colorful, multi-stranded marine rope can be looped through brass rings.*

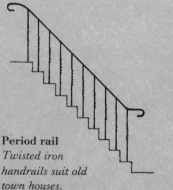

Period rail *Twisted iron handrails suit old town houses.*

WATER

Building a water feature

Small areas of water should be contained in formal water features; the natural pond-look appears contrived in small urban spaces. The detailing of a water feature is all-important – a tacky finish will ruin the overall look which you had planned. Always seek professional advice if you are thinking about installing an electric water pump or constructing a jetty. Once you have a water feature it is important to keep the water clean so it is always clear.

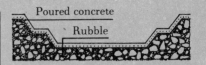

Simple concrete pool *Concrete is a watertight material and ideally suited to the construction of small, formal water features.*

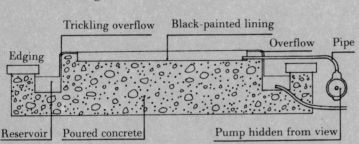

Shallow pool with overflow *A pump (which would, in reality, be hidden from view) pushes water into a shallow pool from which it gently trickles into a lower reservoir. A drainpipe (which should be hidden from view) leads back to the pump and the water is recycled.*

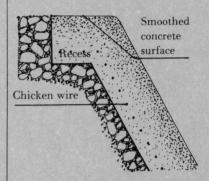

Making a neat finish *To prepare the edges of a concrete pool for an edging recess the concrete into the surrounding tamped rubble.*

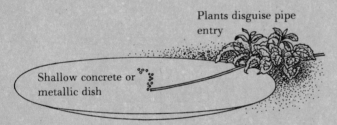

Brimming "dish" pool *Air from a pipe attached to a small pump creates a continuous gentle bubbling in the center of the shallow pool. The pool itself takes the form of a concrete or metallic "dish", sunk slightly into the surrounding subsoil. Disguise the air pipe entry with plants.*

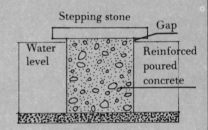

Stepping stones *Stepping stones will enable you to cross a small-space water garden and reach aquatic plants for maintenance.*

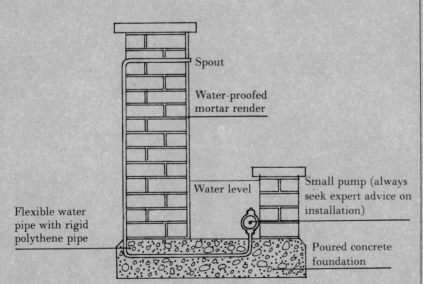

Pool and spout *A small electric pump in the pool pushes water up through a pipe and out of a spout. The water splashes back into the pool and is recycled. Concrete copings give the walls of the water feature walls a neat finish and make a decorative contrast with the brick.*

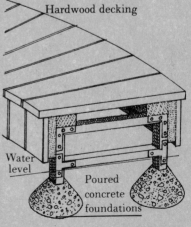

Jetty *Straight or curved low-level jetties should be raised just above water level, on an aluminum frame set in concrete.*

PLANTING DETAILS

Good planting techniques and the careful maintenance of plants are the key to creating the healthy and attractive form of growth that will bring to fruition the imagined results of your planting scheme, whether it be a collection of unusual bamboos and grasses grown in containers, some climbers growing around a doorway or a small water garden.

In a small-space garden, where all plants will be in full view most of the time, the quality of their maintenance is even more noticeable than in a large garden, where some plants may well blend in as part of a distant background and be out of view for much of the time. The drawings on the following pages demonstrate not only how to plant and care for your plants, paying special attention to those techniques that are indispensable in the small-space garden, such as growing plants in containers, but also less usual techniques that are particularly suited to bringing life and interest to confined spaces, such as espalier and cordon training regimes (illustrated on the page opposite).

Many small gardens are surrounded by walls and fences; these are valuable planting areas, and all manner of climbers can be grown up them, supported by wire or trellis where necessary, and small fruit trees can be trained to grow against them. Topiary is another way of bringing interest to a small space — just one or two clipped specimens, grown in containers, may be all you need to bring to life a previously unpromising area like a small front yard.

CLIMBERS

Supporting climbers

Different types of climber need different degrees of support. Clingers adhere to vertical structures with aerial roots and need no extra support system. Twiners have tendrils that need a support system of wires or trellis to entwine. Some climbers, like climbing roses and shrubs that will grow vertically against a wall, need not only a support system but also require tying in to support their bushy form of growth.

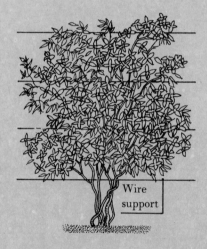

Supporting a twiner *This clematis twines around wires.*

Types of growth
The type of support required by a climber is determined by its method of growth.

A twiner *Plants like this clematis have tendrils.*

A clinger *This ivy has aerial roots.*

Supporting a scrambler *This honeysuckle scrambles up a trellis.*

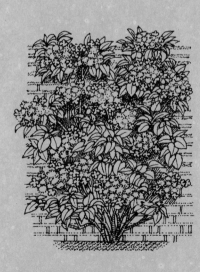

Self-supporting clinger *This hydrangea clings to a wall.*

TRAINING TREES

Espalier

Fruit trees that spread naturally in the open can be trained into highly artificial shapes in the form of cordon or espalier. An espalier consists of a fruit tree with a central vertical stem and evenly-spaced horizontal arms. The tree is shaped by a combination of pruning and training along cane and wire supports.

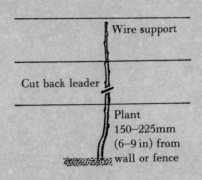

Espalier – first winter *Prune above three healthy buds.*

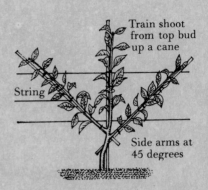

Espalier – first summer *Train shoot and side arms up canes.*

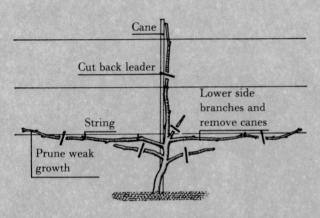

Espalier – second winter *Remove canes and tie arms to wire. Cut back leader and prune weak growth.*

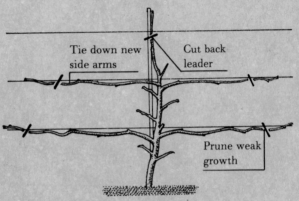

Espalier – third winter *Repeat procedure as in previous season; continue to train the leader up a cane.*

Cordons

A cordon consists of just one stem of a fruit tree trained to grow vertically at an angle of 45 degrees, or two or three trained to grow parallel to one another, so the tree becomes fork-shaped. The cordon form, like the espalier, is an excellent way of growing fruit trees in a small garden which is enclosed by walls or fences.

Cordon – first year (right) *Plant the tree in spring. Attach a leader to a cane at 45 degrees. If the young tree has laterals, prune those over 150mm (6 in) long to four buds. Thereafter prune the tree each summer.*

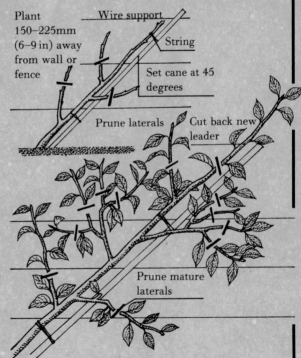

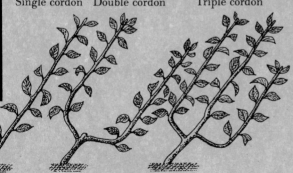

Styles of cordon *Whichever style of cordon you choose fruit will always be within easy reach.*

Cordon – summer pruning *Cut back the leader to 25mm (1 in) and prune mature shoots and sub-laterals.*

PLANTING SHRUBS

Planting technique

Ideally, shrubs should be planted in their dormant period. Dig a hole large enough to accommodate the bare roots or root ball (loosen roots of a container-grown shrub).

Excavated soil   Hole large enough for root spread

Growing medium

Digging *Excavate a suitable size hole and thoroughly turn the soil, adding a little growing medium.*

Bare-rooted shrub

Trim broken or damaged roots

Preparation *Trim damaged roots (if a container-grown plant is pot-bound gently tease out its roots).*

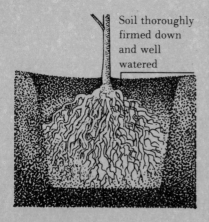

Soil thoroughly firmed down and well watered

Planting *Ensure you spread the roots of bare-root plants, place in the hole, backfill and firm down.*

PRUNING SHRUBS

Why prune?

Pruning your shrubs will enable you to regulate their height and

Shape before pruning

Soft-wood shrub – pruned shape
Prune soft-wood shrubs, like this Buddleia sp., hard each spring.

Soft-wood shrub – new growth
Rather than becoming ungainly the shrub will have a neat shape.

shape, particularly important in a small garden. It will also improve the quality of their growth and determine the level at which they flower. Prune shrubs after they have finished flowering.

Shape after pruning

Woody shrub – pruned shape
Prune woody shrubs, like this Philadelphus sp., after flowering.

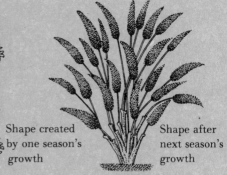

Shape created by one season's growth

Shape after next season's growth

Woody shrub – new growth
Instead of becoming leggy the shrub will have a rounded shape.

PERENNIALS

Rejuvenating perennials

Perennials require a certain amount of maintenance, for if left to grow untended for many seasons they become large and

untidy in shape and their quality of growth becomes poorer and poorer, until they eventually die. To rejuvenate perennials divide them after flowering, using a spade for tuberous perennials and two forks for fibrous ones (the latter is illustrated below).

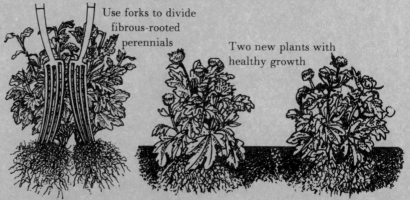

Use forks to divide fibrous-rooted perennials

Two new plants with healthy growth

Dividing *When plants need rejuvenation, lift and divide them (in autumn). You will now have several plants instead of one and these can be newly planted. Prepare the soil as for a shrub. After a few seasons divide the new plants.*

TOPIARY

Clipping plants of dense growth

Evergreen hedging plants, such as box (*Buxus semper-virens*) and privet (*Ligustrum ovalifolium*), can be clipped into artificial shapes. To create the neat, tailored look that characterizes topiary, the shrub should be clipped three to four times a year during its early life; when mature, once or twice a year should be adequate. Clip during the growing period, using well-sharpened tools. (See p.216 for a list of evergreen shrubs suitable for topiary.)

Clipping plants of loose growth

Flowering plants with a naturally loose shape of growth, such as fuchsia and *Pelargonium* spp., can be pruned and trained so they bush out in a rounded shape, above a bare stem (this shape is known as a mop-headed standard). See page 216 for a list of plants suitable for pruning to this shape. Plants shaped like this look particularly effective if grown in pots; since many of them need protection from the frost, growing them in pots also makes it easy to move them to a sheltered position in the winter. Artificially-shaped flowering plants make an elegant summer feature for small-space gardens.

Correct shape *Aim always to create shapes that slope outwards and downwards, broadly following the natural growth of the plant.*

Incorrect shape *Do not create the broadest area at the top as snow will collect on top of it and light will not reach the lower areas.*

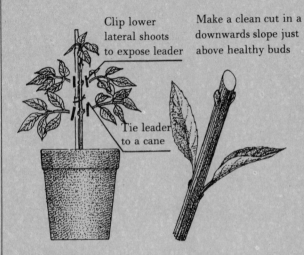

Clip lower lateral shoots to expose leader

Make a clean cut in a downwards slope just above healthy buds

Tie leader to a cane

Pruning lower growth *Clip off the lower lateral shoots as they appear, in order to expose the lower stem (which should be supported with a cane).*

Pruning upper growth *To encourage the top of the plant to bush out, remove the lateral shoots at the top of the stem, cutting just above the new buds.*

Sphere *This traditional shape is well suited to plants grown in containers, giving a balanced look. Clip the side shoots to expose the main stem of the plant.*

Geometrical point *To give a plant a symmetrical shape, use a string guiding line to help cut slopes which fall accurately away from the vertical of the plant.*

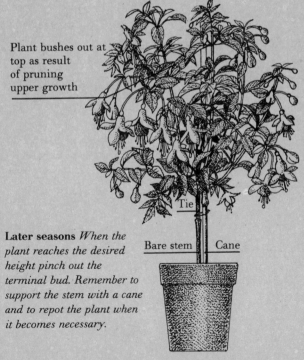

Plant bushes out at top as result of pruning upper growth

Tie

Bare stem   Cane

Arch *Curves are easier to cut than straight lines. Arch-shaped plants will receive an optimum amount of light and moisture.*

Later seasons *When the plant reaches the desired height pinch out the terminal bud. Remember to support the stem with a cane and to repot the plant when it becomes necessary.*

Using wire shapes

Hedging plants of dense growth such as privet (*Ligustrum ovalifolium*) can be clipped to shape as they grow through a preformed, meshed wire shape.

Climbing plants, such as ivy (*Hedera* spp.) and creeping fig (*Ficus pumila*) and other plants (see p.216) can be trained to grow up and around wire shapes. Simple designs look best.

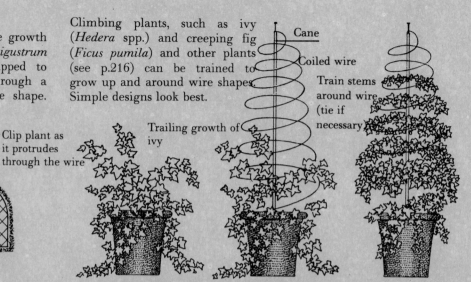

Cane

Coiled wire

Train stems around wire (tie if necessary)

Trailing growth of ivy

Clip plant as it protrudes through the wire

Preformed wire shape

Growing through wire *A topiary method for hedging plants.*

Growing up a wire shape *The branches should be tied loosely to the wire. Position trailing plants around the edges of the wire and vertical plants centrally.*

PLANTS IN GRAVEL

Using gravel

Consolidated gravel can be used instead of paving, and plants can be grown through it.

Making a planting pocket *As well as allowing self-seeders to grow in the dust in a gravel surface, you can dig a hole through the layers beneath to create a planting pocket.*

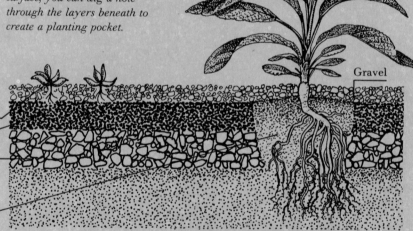

Gravel

Self-seeders growing in dust in the gravel

Sand and gravel

Tamped rubble

Planting pocket made by piercing the layers with a crowbar

CONTAINERS

Preparation and care

Make sure your container has drainage holes; cover these with a layer of crocks or pebbles and a layer of growing medium (soil or purchased soilless mix). Arrange your plants (or plant) on these layers so their roots touch the growing medium and their crowns are just below the rim. Backfill with the growing medium and water well.

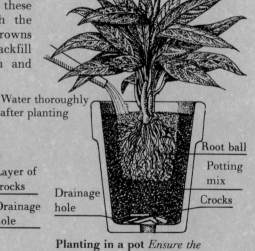

Water thoroughly after planting

Root ball

Potting mix

Crocks

Drainage hole

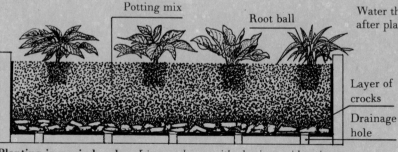

Potting mix

Root ball

Layer of crocks

Drainage hole

Planting in a window-box *Line wooden and terracotta window-boxes with plastic, to aid moisture retention of the growing medium.*

Planting in a pot *Ensure the plant is large enough for the roots.*

Hanging baskets

Hanging baskets can be lined with moss, or a man-made porous material. Always use a good-quality mixture that will retain moisture.

Moss lining

Man-made lining

Vertical plant

Trailing plant

Potting mix

AUTOMATIC IRRIGATION

The advantages

Plants grown in pots need more watering than those grown in beds. An automatic irrigation system is a great time-saver if you have many pots and will ensure your plants' survival when you are away for any time.

The system (right and below) *Automatic irrigation systems consist of a time-switched valve that regulates the flow of water from a tap which is left on, right, and a hose with small outlets that lies over the pots, below.*

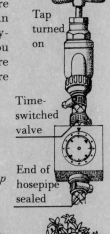

Tap turned on

Time-switched valve

End of hosepipe sealed

PLANTING IN WATER

Planting methods

Rather than covering the bottom of your water feature with soil, grow water plants in soil-filled containers for this will give you control over your plants and make cleaning your pool easier.

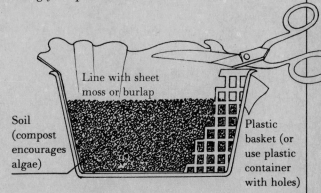

Line with sheet moss or burlap

Soil (compost encourages algae)

Plastic basket (or use plastic container with holes)

Preparation *Line a basket and fill with garden soil (do not use commercial potting mixes or soil).*

Basket

Gravel

Lining

Soil

Planting *Firm the plant in well. A layer of pea gravel or small pebbles will prevent the soil floating away when the planting basket is submerged in the water.*

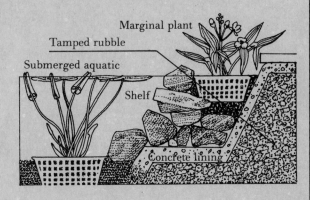

Marginal plant

Tamped rubble

Submerged aquatic

Shelf

Concrete lining

Positioning *Marginal plants should be placed on a submerged shelf so only their roots and some of their stem are in water. Aquatics, such as water lilies, should be placed on a submerged shelf when they are young and lowered in gradual stages to the pool floor as they grow.*

SMALL-GARDEN PLANT GUIDE

In this plant guide the abbreviation spp. (species) is used to cover species *and* cultivars of the generic name it follows.

Betula pendula (Silver birch)

SHADE-TOLERANT PLANTS

DRY SHADE

Trees
Acer negundo Box elder
Acer palmatum Japanese maple
Betula pendula Silver birch
Caragana arborescens Siberian pea tree
Carpinus betulus Hornbeam
Ilex spp. Holly
Quercus spp. (smaller forms) Oak
Robinia spp. (except *R.* 'Frisia')
Sorbus aria Common whitebeam
Sorbus vilmorinii Whitebeam

Shrubs and perennials
Ajuga spp. Bugle
Aucuba spp.
Berberis spp. Barberry
Bergenia spp.
Brunnera macrophylla
Buxus sempervirens Common box
Centranthus ruber Valerian
Cotoneaster spp.
Cyclamen coum
Cyclamen hederifolium

Epimedium spp.
Euphorbia robbiae Spurge
Garrya elliptica
Geranium macrorrhizum Crane's-bill
Geranium pratense Crane's-bill
Geranium sanguineum Crane's-bill
Hedera helix 'Goldheart' English ivy
Helleborus foetidus Stinking hellebore
Hemerocallis spp. Day lily
Ilex spp. Holly
Iris foetidissima Stinking iris
Lamium spp. Deadnettle
Liriope muscari Lily turf
Lonicera pileata Honeysuckle
Lunaria spp. Honesty
Mahonia aquifolium Oregon grape
Osmanthus heterophyllus
Pachysandra terminalis
Polygonatum spp. Solomon's seal
Prunus laurocerasus Common laurel
Pulmonaria spp. Lungwort
Rhus typhina Stag's horn sumach
Ribes sanguineum Flowering currant
Ruscus aculeatus Butcher's broom
Sambucus racemosa Red-berried elder
Skimmia japonica
Smyrnium spp. Horse parsley
Symphoricarpos albus Snowberry
Tiarella cordifolia Foam flower
Tolmiea menziesii Pickaback
Vinca minor Myrtle
Viola labradorica Violet
Waldsteinia fragarioides

MOIST SHADE

Trees
Acer griseum Paperbark maple
Acer japonicum Full-moon maple

Acer palmatum Japanese maple
Acer pseudoplatanus 'Brilliantissimum' Sycamore
Alnus spp. Alder
Betula nigra River birch
Cornus nuttallii Dogwood
Crataegus spp. Hawthorn
Davidia involucrata Dove tree
Fraxinus spp. Ash
Laburnum × watereri Golden chain tree
Populus spp. Poplar
Prunus padus Bird cherry
Pterocarya spp. Wingnut
Quercus spp. (smaller forms) Oak
Salix spp. Willow
Stewartia pseudocamellia

Shrubs and perennials
Alchemilla mollis Lady's mantle
Aruncus dioicus Goat's beard
Astilbe spp. False goat's beard
Aucuba japonica 'Picturata' Japanese laurel
Aucuba japonica 'Salicifolia' Japanese laurel
Aucuba japonica 'Variegata' Spotted laurel
Caltha palustris Marsh marigold
Camellia spp.
Clerodendrum trichotomum
Clethra alnifolia 'Paniculata' Sweet pepper bush
Cornus spp. Dogwood
Elaeagnus commutata Silverberry
Elaeagnus angustifolia
Elaeagnus umbellata
Filipendula ulmaria 'Aurea' Queen of the meadow
Fothergilla monticola
Gaultheria procumbens Wintergreen
Gunnera manicata
Hamamelis spp. Witch hazel
Hedera spp. Ivy
Helleborus spp. Hellebore
Hemerocallis spp. Day lily
Hosta spp. Plantain lily
Hydrangea spp.

Ligularia spp.
Ligustrum spp. Privet
Liriope muscari Lily turf
Lythrum spp. Loosestrife
Osmanthus spp.
Pachysandra terminalis
Peltiphyllum peltatum
Pernettya spp.
Pieris spp. Andromeda
Polygonum spp. Knotgrass
Rheum palmatum Ornamental rhubarb
Rhododendron spp.
Sambucus spp. Elder
Sarcococca humilis Sweet box
Skimmia japonica
Staphylea spp. Bladdernut
Symphoricarpos sp. Snowberry
Viburnum davidii
Viburnum opulus
Viburnum rhytidophyllum
Vinca minor Myrtle

PLANTS FOR DRY SITES IN FULL SUN

Abelia sp.
Acanthus spinosus Bear's breeches
Achillea spp. Yarrow
Agapanthus spp. African lily
Alstroemeria aurantiaca Peruvian lily
Anaphalis triplinervis
Artemisia 'Silver Mound'
Artemisia 'Silver Queen'
Aurinia saxatilis Gold dust
Berberis spp. Barberry
Bergenia cordifolia
Buddleia davidii Butterfly bush
Buddleia fallowiana Butterfly bush
Buxus sempervirens Common box
Catananche caerulea 'Major'
Ceanothus spp.
Centaurea dealbata 'John Coutts' Cornflower
Ceratostigma willmottianum
Cistus spp. Rock rose
Colutea arborescens Bladder senna
Corokia cotoneaster
Coronilla valentina glauca
Cortaderia spp. Pampas grass

Cotoneaster horizontalis
Crambe cordifolia
Crocosmia masonorum
Cytisus spp. Broom
Dianthus spp. Pink
Echinops ritro Globe thistle
Euonymus fortunei
Geranium spp. Crane's-bill
Gypsophila spp. Baby's breath
Hebe spp. Veronica
Helianthemum spp. Sun rose
Helichrysum lanatum
Hibiscus syriacus Rose of Sharon
Hippophae rhamnoides Sea buckthorn
Holcus mollis 'Variegatus' Creeping velvet grass
Hypericum spp. St John's wort
Incarvillea delavayi Trumpet flower
Indigofera gerardiana
Iris foetidissima Stinking iris
Iris germanica Iris
Iris pallida dalmatica 'Argenteo-variegata' Iris
Kniphofia spp. Red hot poker
Kolkwitzia amabilis 'Pink Cloud' Beauty bush
Lavandula spp. Lavender
Lespedeza thunbergii
Libertia formosa
Nandina domestica Heavenly bamboo
Nepeta × faassenii Catmint
Nerine bowdenii

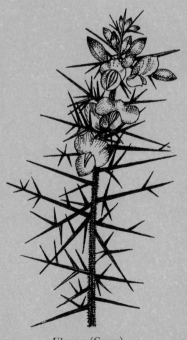

Ulex sp. (Gorse)

Oenothera spp. Evening primrose
Papaver orientale Oriental poppy
Penstemon barbatus Beard-tongue
Perovskia atriplicifolia 'Blue Spire' Russian sage
Philadelphus spp. Mock orange
Phlox subulata
Phormium tenax New Zealand flax
Potentilla tabernaemontani Spring cinquefoil
Ribes spp. Flowering currant
Rosmarinus officinalis Rosemary
Salidago spp. Golden rod
Salvia spp. Sage
Sambucus spp. Elder
Santolina spp. Lavender cotton
Saponaria ocymoides Soapwort
Sedum spp. Stonecrop
Sempervivum spp. Houseleek
Senecio spp.
Sisyrinchium striatum Blue-eyed grass
Sophora tetraptera Kowhai
Spartium junceum Spanish broom
Spiraea spp. Bridal wreath
Stachys lanata Lamb's ears
Stipa spp. Needlegrass
Tamarix spp. Tamarisk
Teucrium chamaedrys Germander
Thymus spp. Thyme
Ulex spp. Gorse
Verbascum spp. Mullein
Viola hederacea Australian violet
Yucca spp. Spanish bayonet
Zauschneria californica Californian fuchsia

PLANTS FOR EXPOSED SITES

HOT, DRY, WINDY CONDITIONS

Berberis buxifolia 'Nana' Barberry
Berberis candidula 'Amstelveen' Barberry

Berberis 'Parkjuweel'
  Barberry
Berberis × *stenophylla*
  Barberry
Berberis thunbergii
  'Atropurpurea Nana'
  Barberry
Berberis thunbergii 'Aurea'
  Golden barberry
Chamaecyparis lawsoniana
  Lawson cypress
Chamaecyparis obtusa
  'Tetragona Aurea' Hinoki
  cypress
Chamaecyparis pisifera
  'Boulevard' Sawara
  cypress
Cistus spp. Rock rose
Cytisus spp. Broom
Erica spp. Heath
Gaultheria procumbens
  Checkerberry
Genista hispanica Spanish broom
Genista lydia Bulgarian broom
Genista pilosa Broom
Genista tinctoria Dyer's
  greenwood
Juniperus chinensis 'Blaauw'
  Juniper
Juniperus communis
  'Compressa' Common juniper
Juniperus communis
  'Depressed Star' Common
  juniper
Juniperus communis
  'Hornibrookii' Common
  juniper
Juniperus conferta Shore
  juniper
Juniperus horizontalis
  'Turquoise Spreader'
  Creeping juniper
Juniperus horizontalis 'Glauca'
  Creeping juniper
Juniperus horizontalis
  'Wiltonii' Creeping juniper
Juniperus sabina
  'Tamariscifolia' Juniper
Juniperus virginiana Red
  cedar
Lavandula spp. Lavender
Picea pungens 'Compacta'
  Colorado spruce
Pinus mugo Mountain pine
Rosmarinus officinalis
  Rosemary
Ruscus aculeatus
Santolina pinnata Cotton
  lavender

Berberis sp. (Barberry)

Spartium junceum Spanish
  broom
Syringa patula Lilac
Taxus baccata 'Standishii' Yew
Thuja occidentalis 'Rheingold'
  White cedar
Thuja orientalis 'Aurea Nana'
  Chinese arbor-vitae
Viburnum davidii

COLD, DRY, WINDY CONDITIONS

Acer campestre Hedge maple
Acer negundo Ash-leaved
  maple, Box elder
Berberis spp. Barberry
Betula papyrifera Canoe
  birch
Buddleia alternifolia Butterfly
  bush
Chaenomeles spp. Flowering
  quince
Cornus racemosa Gray
  dogwood
Corylus spp. Hazel
Cotoneaster spp.
Crataegus spp. Ornamental
  thorn
Cupressus arizonica Arizona
  cypress
Cupressus macrocarpa
  'Goldcrest' Monterey
  cypress
Deutzia spp.
Elaeagnus angustifolia
Euonymus spp. (evergreen
  varieties)

Ilex glabra Ink berry
Juniperus chinensis 'Pfitzeriana
  Aurea' Juniper
Juniperus communis
  'Depressed Star' Common
  juniper
Juniperus communis
  'Hornibrookii' Common
  juniper
Juniperus conferta Shore
  juniper
Juniperus horizontalis 'Bar
  Harbor' Creeping juniper
Juniperus horizontalis 'Glauca'
  Creeping juniper
Juniperus horizontalis
  'Plumosa Aurea' Creeping
  juniper
Juniperus horizontalis
  'Wiltonii' Creeping juniper
Juniperus sabina
  'Tamariscifolia' Juniper
Juniperus squamata 'Blue
  Carpet' Juniper
Juniperus squamata 'Blue Star'
  Juniper
Juniperus squamata 'Meyeri'
  Juniper
Juniperus virginiana 'Grey
  Owl' Pencil cedar
Kerria japonica Japanese
  kerria
Laburnum spp. Golden chain
  tree
Pachysandra terminalis
Philadelphus spp. Mock
  orange
Pinus mugo Mountain pine
Pittosporum spp.
Potentilla spp. Cinquefoil
Sorbus spp.
Spiraea spp.
Tamarix spp. Tamarisk
Vaccinium pallidum Blueberry
Viburnum lantana Wayfaring
  tree

VERTICAL PLANTING

FAST-GROWING CLIMBERS FOR SCREENING

Actinidia chinensis Chinese
  gooseberry
Akebia quinata

Campsis grandiflora Trumpet
vine
Clematis montana
Clematis paniculata
Hedera helix cvs. English ivy
Humulus lupulus 'Aureus' Hop
Jasminum officinale Common
white jasmine
Lonicera japonica 'Halliana'
Japanese honeysuckle
Lonicera periclymenum
'Belgica' Early Dutch
honeysuckle
Lonicera periclymenum
'Sempervirens' Trumpet
honeysuckle
Parthenocissus quinquefolia
Virginia creeper
Polygonum aubertii Silver
fleece vine
Polygonum baldschuanicum
Russian vine
Vitis coignetiae Japanese
crimson glory vine
Vitis 'Brant' Grape vine
Wisteria sinensis Chinese
wisteria

EVERGREEN CLIMBERS FOR YEAR-ROUND EFFECT

Bignonia capreolata Cross vine
Hedera spp. Ivy
Lonicera etrusca (semi-
evergreen)
Lonicera japonica Japanese
honeysuckle (semi-
evergreen)

SHRUBS FOR MILD CLIMATES OR WALL PROTECTION

Abeliophyllum distichum
Abutilon megapotamicum
Acacia dealbata Silver wattle
Azara microphylla
Buddleia colvilei Butterfly
bush
Buddleia fallowiana Butterfly
bush
Camellia spp.
Ceanothus spp.
Chaenomeles speciosa
Japanese quince

Vitis coignetiae
(Japanese crimson glory vine)

Chimonanthus praecox Winter
sweet
Corylopsis spp. Winter hazel
Cytisus battandieri Moroccan
broom
Daphne odora Winter daphne
Elaeagnus pungens
Escallonia spp.
Forsythia spp.
Fremontodendron californicum
Fremontia
Fuchsia spp.
Garrya elliptica
Hebe 'Gauntletti' Veronica
Hebe 'Midsummer Beauty'
Veronica
Hebe 'La Seduisante'
Veronica
Hebe 'Veitchii' Veronica
Itea illicifolia
Leptospermum scoparium
'Nicholsii' Tea tree
Leptospermum scoparium 'Red
Damask' Tea tree
Lippia citriodora Lemon-
scented verbena
Magnolia grandiflora
'Exmouth'
Myrtus communis Common
myrtle
Phygelius capensis
Prunus lusitanica Portugal
laurel
Robinia hispida Rose acacia
Rosa (some varieties) Rose
Solanum jasminoides Potato
vine

Viburnum × *burkwoodii* 'Park
Farm Hybrid'
Viburnum tinus Laurustinus

PLANTS RESISTANT TO LIMITED ATMOSPHERIC POLLUTION

Trees
Acer negundo Ash-leaved
maple, box elder
Ailanthus altissima Tree of
heaven
Amelanchier spp. Shadblow
Aralia elata Japanese angelica
Betula pendula Silver birch
Carpinus spp. Hornbeam
Crataegus spp. Hawthorn
Eucalyptus spp. Gum tree
Fraxinus oxycarpa Ash
Gleditsia spp.
Magnolia kobus
Malus spp. Crab apple
Prunus spp. Cherry
Pyrus salicifolia 'Pendula'
Willow-leaved pear
Quercus phellos Willow oak
Robinia spp. False acacia
Sorbus spp. Mountain ash oak
Zelkova serrata

Conifers
Cryptoemeria japonica
Japanese cedar
Ginkgo biloba Maidenhair tree
Juniperus chinensis 'Old Gold'
Juniper
Juniperus chinensis 'Pfitzeriana
Glauca' Juniper
Juniperus squamata 'Blue
Carpet' Juniper
Juniperus squamata 'Blue Star'
Juniper
Juniperus squamata 'Meyeri'
Juniper
Juniperus virginiana 'Grey
Owl' Pencil cedar
Taxus baccata 'Aurea' Yew
Taxus baccata 'Fastigiata' Irish
yew
Taxus baccata 'Semperaurea'
Yew

Shrubs
Aesculus parviflora Bottlebrush
buckeye

Arundinaria spp. Bamboo
Berberis spp. Barberry
Buddleia spp. Butterfly bush
Buxus sempervirens Common
  box
Camellia spp.
Ceratostigma willmottianum
Cistus spp. Rock rose
Clethra alnifolia Sweet pepper
  bush
Colutea arborescens Bladder
  senna
Cornus spp. Dogwood
Corylus maxima Hazel
Cotinus coggygria Smoke tree
Cotoneaster spp.
Cytisus spp. Broom
Deutzia spp.
Elaeagnus spp.
Erica spp. Heath
Escallonia spp.
Euonymus spp.
Fatsia japonica
Forsythia spp.
Genista spp. Broom
Hedera colchica Persian ivy
Hedera helix English ivy
Hibiscus syriacus Tree mallow
Hydrangea spp.
Hypericum spp. St John's wort
Ilex glabra Inkberry
Kerria japonica
Kolkwitzia amabilis 'Pink
  Cloud' Beauty bush
Leycesteria formosa
  Himalayan honeysuckle
Lonicera pileata Honeysuckle
Magnolia spp.
Mahonia spp. Oregon grape
Olearia × haastii Daisy bush

Magnolia sp.

Osmanthus spp.
Pernettya spp.
Philadelphus spp. Mock
  orange
Physocarpus opulifolius
Potentilla spp. Cinquefoil
Prunus laurocerasus Portugal
  laurel
Pyracantha spp. Firethorn
Rhododendron hardy hybrids
Rhus spp. Sumac
Ribes sanguineum Flowering
  currant
Rubus 'Benenden'
Salix spp. Willow
Sambucus spp. Elder
Sarcococca humilis Sweet box
Senecio 'Sunshine'
Skimmia spp.
Spartium junceum Spanish
  broom
Spiraea spp.
Staphylea spp. Bladdernut
Stephanandra incisa 'Crispa'
Stranvaesia spp.
Symphoricarpos spp.
  Snowberry
Syringa spp. Lilac
Tamarix tetrandra Tamarisk
Ulex spp. Gorse
Viburnum opulus Guelder rose
Viburnum tinus Laurustinus
Vinca major Greater
  periwinkle
Weigela spp.

PLANTS TO FILTER NOISE

Ailanthus altissima Tree of
  heaven
Buxus sempervirens Common
  box
Carpinus betulus 'Fastigiata'
  Hornbeam
Cupressocyparis leylandii
  Leyland cypress
Fagus sylvatica Beech
Ilex spp. Holly
Pinus spp. Pine
Pterocarya fraxinifolia
Rhododendron compact hybrids
Taxus baccata Yew
Thuja occidentalis 'Rheingold'
  White cedar
Viburnum rhytidophyllum

GROUND COVER PLANTS

LOW-GROWING GROUND COVER

Aegopodium podagraria
  Goatweed
Acaena spp.
Ajuga spp. Bugle
Alchemilla spp. Lady's mantle
Arctostaphylos uva-ursi
  Bearberry
Armeria maritima Thrift
Asarum europeum European
  wild ginger
Aubrieta spp. Rock cress
Bergenia spp.
Convallaria majalis Lily-of-
  the-valley
Cotoneaster dammeri
Cotoneaster horizontalis
Dianthus spp. Pink
Epimedium spp.
Erica carnea Heath
Euonymus fortunei
Gaultheria procumbens
  Checkerberry
Hedera helix Ivy
Helianthemum spp. Sun rose
Heuchera sanguinea Coral
  bells
Hosta spp. Plantain lily
Hypericum calycinum
  Creeping St John's wort
Iberis spp. Candytuft
Juniperus horizantalis
  Creeping juniper
Lamium maculatum Dead
  nettle
Nepeta spp. Catmint
Phlox subulata Creeping phlox
Polygonum spp. Knotweed
Pulmonaria spp. Lungwort
Ruta graveolens Rue
Santolina spp. Lavender cotton
Saponaria ocymoides Soapwort
Saponaria × olivana Soapwort
Saxifraga spp.
Sedum spp. Stonecrop
Stachys lanata Lamb's ears
Teucrium chamaedrys
  Germander
Thymus spp. Thyme
Vinca major Greater
  periwinkle
Vinca minor Myrtle

Viola spp. Violet
Zauschneria californica
 California fuchsia

PLANTS FOR A COUNTRY LOOK

Shrubs

Amelanchier alnifolia
 Serviceberry
Berberis spp. Barberry
Buddleia davidii Butterfly
 bush
Buxus sempervirens Common
 box
Chaenomeles spp. Ornamental
 quince
Clethra alnifolia Summer
 sweet
Cistus spp. Rock rose
Cornus alba Red-barked
 dogwood
Crataegus monogyna
 Hawthorn
Cytisus scoparius Scotch broom
Daphne spp.
Hippophae rhamnoides Sea
 buckthorn
Jasminum spp. Jasmine
Juniperus communis Common
 juniper
Lavandula spp.
 Lavender
Lonicera periclymenum
 Honeysuckle
Philadelphus spp. Mock
 orange
Rosa (shrubby types) Rose
Rosmarinus officinalis
 Rosemary
Sambucus spp. Elder
Syringa spp. Lilac
Viburnum spp.

Annuals and perennials

Achillea spp. Yarrow
Alcea spp. Hollyhock
Amelanchier ovalis
 Serviceberry
Anchusa spp. Alkanet
Antirrhinum spp. Snapdragon
Aster spp. Michaelmas daisy
Aurinia saxatilis 'Gold dust'
Berberis spp. Barberry
Cardamine pratensis Cuckoo-
 flower
Centaurea cyanus Cornflower

Juniperus communis (Common juniper)

Centaurea nigra Hardheads
Cheiranthus spp. Wallflower
Cirsium vulgare Spear thistle
Colchicum spp. Autumn crocus
Colutea spp. Bladder senna
Cosmos spp.
Delphinium spp. Larkspur
Dianthus barbatus Sweet
 William
Digitalis purpurea Foxglove
Echinops spp. Globe thistle
Endymion non-scriptus
 Bluebell
Fragaria vesca Wild
 strawberry
Godetia spp.
Helianthemum nummularium
 Rock rose
Helianthus annuus Sunflower
Hyssopus officinalis Hyssop
Iberis sempervirens Candytuft
Lathyrus latifolius Everlasting
 pea
Lippia citriodora Verbena
Lobelia erinus
Lobularia maritima Sweet
 alyssum
Lunaria annua Honesty
Lupinus spp. Lupin
Lychnis flos-cuculi Ragged
 robin
Lythrum salicaria Purple
 loosestrife
Malva sylvestris Common
 mallow
Matthiola bicornis Night-
 scented stock
Myosotis arvensis Field forget-
 me-not
Narcissus spp. Daffodil
Nepeta cataria Catmint

Nicotiana spp. Tobacco plant
Nigella damascena Love-in-
 a-mist
Oenothera biennis Evening
 primrose
Petunia spp.
Phlox paniculata
Plantago lanceolata Ribwort
 plantain
Primula veris Primrose
Pulmonaria officinalis
 Lungwort
Ranunculus ficaria Lesser
 celandine
Reseda lutea Mignonette
Salvia spp. Sage
Saponaria officinalis Soapwort
Scabiosa spp. Scabious
Sedum spectabile Ice plant
Solidago spp. Goldenrod
Thymus spp. Thyme
Trifolium repens White clover
Tropaeolum spp. Nasturtium
Tulipa spp. Tulip
Valeriana spp. Valerian
Verbascum nigrum Dark
 mullein
Veronica spp. Speedwell
Viola spp. Pansy, violet, viola

PLANTS OF ARCHITECTURAL MERIT

Trees

Acer japonicum Japanese
 maple
Ailanthus altissima Tree of
 heaven
Catalpa bignonioides 'Aurea'
 Indian bean tree
Rhus typhina Stag's horn sumac
Robinia pseudoacacia 'Frisia'
 False acacia

Shrubs

Acer palmatum Japanese
 maple
Aralia elata Angelica tree
Arundinaria palmata Bamboo
Clerodendrum trichotomum
Cordyline australis New
 Zealand cabbage tree
Euonymus alatus Winged
 euonymus

Fatshedera lizei
Fatsia japonica
Magnolia grandiflora
Mahonia japonica
Paeonia delavayi Tree peony
Paeonia lutea ludlowii Tree peony
Phormium tenax New Zealand flax
Poncirus trifoliata Hardy orange
Romneya coulteri Tree poppy
Viburnum davidii
Viburnum rhytidophyllum
Yucca spp. Spanish bayonet

Perennials
Acanthus spp. Bear's breeches
Arum italicum 'Pictum' Lords-and-ladies
Bergenia spp.
Eryngium spp. Sea holly
Euphorbia wulfenii Spurge
Gunnera sp.
Helleborus foetidus Stinking hellebore
Helleborus lividus corsicus Corsican hellebore
Hosta spp. Plantain lily
Iris foetidissima Stinking iris
Iris pallida 'Aurea Variegata'
Kniphofia spp. Red hot poker
Libertia spp.
Ligularia spp.
Onopordum spp. Thistle
Peltiphyllum peltatum Umbrella plant
Rheum palmatum Ornamental rhubarb
Rodgersia spp.
Salvia argentea Silver sage
Sedum spp. Stonecrop
Silybum marianum Holy thistle
Sisyrinchium striatum
Stipa gigantea Feather grass

PLANTS FOR COLOR

TREES AND SHRUBS FOR AUTUMN LEAF COLOR

Acer spp. Maple
Amelanchier spp. Shadblow
Aronia arbutifolia Chokeberry

Eryngium sp. (Sea holly)

Berberis koreana Barberry
Berberis thunbergii Japanese barberry
Cercidiphyllum japonicum Katsura tree
Cornus florida Flowering dogwood
Cornus kousa Chinese dogwood
Cornus nuttallii Mountain dogwood
Enkianthus campanulatus Redvein enkianthus
Euonymus alatus Winged euonymus
Hydrangea quercifolia Oakleaf hydrangea
Oxydendrum arboreum Oakleaf hydrangea
Parrotia persica
Prunus spp. Flowering cherry
Sorbus spp. Mountain ash
Vaccinium spp. Blueberry

PLANTS FOR WINTER TO SPRING INTEREST

Trees and shrubs
Acer palmatum 'Senkaki' (stem) Japanese maple
Camellia sasanqua (flower)
Chimonanthus praecox (flower) Winter sweet
Cornus spp. (stem) Dogwood
Cornus mas (flower) Cornelian cherry
Corylopsis spp. (flower) Winter hazel
Corylus avellana (catkin) Hazel
Erica carnea (flowers of some forms) Winter heath

Hamamelis spp. (flower)
Lonicera fragrantissima (flower) Winter honeysuckle
Mahonia japonica (flower)
Parrotia persica (flower) Persian ironwood
Prunus subhirtella 'Autumnalis' (flower) Spring cherry
Salix caprea (catkin) Pussy willow
Sarcococca spp. (flower) Sweet box

Perennials
Bergenia spp.
Crocus spp.
Eranthis hyemalis
Galanthus spp. Snowdrops
Helleborus spp. Hellebore
Iris histrioides
Narcissus (early varieties)
Narcissus 'February Gold'
Narcissus 'Forerunner'
Pulmonaria rubra Lungwort
Tulipa (early varieties)

UNUSUAL FLOWER COLOR

Green flowers
Alchemilla mollis Lady's mantle
Euphorbia wulfenii Spurge
Euphorbia robbiae Spurge
Galtonia viridiflora Summer hyacinth
Helleborus foetidus Stinking hellebore
Helleborus lividus corsicus Corsican hellebore
Iris foetidissima Stinking iris
Lilium 'Limelight'
Molucella laevis Bells of Ireland
Nicotiana alata 'Lime Green' Tobacco plant

Brown flowers
Eremurus hybrids Foxtail lily
Iris 'Solid Mahogany'
Parrotia persica
Sycopsis sinensis

Purple-black flowers
Fritillaria persica
Iris 'Black Swan'
Tulipa 'Black Parrot' Tulip

SCENTED PLANTS

PLANTS WITH SCENTED FLOWERS

Buddleia alternifolia Butterfly bush
Buddleia fallowiana 'Lochinch' Butterfly bush
Cheiranthus spp. Wallflower
Chimonanthus praecox Winter sweet
Clethra alnifolia Summersweet
Convallaria majalis Lily-of-the-valley
Cytisus battandieri Moroccan broom
Daphne spp.
Dianthus barbatus Sweet William
Dianthus spp. Modern pinks and old-fashioned pinks
Genista aetnensis Mount Etna broom
Hamamelis spp. Witch hazel
Heliotropium × *hybridum* Heliotrope
Hyacinthus spp. Hyacinth
Iris bearded hybrids
Jasminum officinale Common white jasmine
Lathyrus odoratus Sweet pea
Lavandula angustifolia Lavender
Ligustrum ovalifolium Golden privet
Lilium auratum Gold-banded lily
Lilium Aurelian hybrids

Lilium candidum Madonna lily
Lilium regale
Lonicera fragrantissima Winter honeysuckle
Lonicera japonica 'Halliana' Japanese honeysuckle
Lonicera periclymenum Honeysuckle
Magnolia sinensis
Magnolia × *soulangiana*
Magnolia virginiana
Malus 'Profusion' Flowering crab
Matthiola incana Stock
Narcissus poeticus Poet's narcissus
Nicotiana alata Tobacco plant
Philadelphus 'Belle Etoilé'
Philadelphus coronarius 'Aureus' Mock orange
Phlox paniculata Summer phlox
Reseda odorata Mignonette
Robinia pseudoacacia 'Frisia' False acacia
Rosa (fragrant cultivars) Rose
Syringa spp. Lilac
Verbena × *hybrida*
Viburnum × *bodnantense*
Viburnum × *burkwoodii*
Viburnum carlesii

PLANTS FOR EVENING SCENT

Heliotropium × *hybridum* Heliotrope
Jasminum officinale Common white jasmine
Lilium auratum
Lilium regale
Matthiola bicornis Night-scented stock
Nicotiana alata Tobacco plant
Nicotiana sylvestris Tobacco plant
Petunia hybrids
Rosa eglanteria Eglantine
Reseda odorata Mignonette

PLANTS WITH AROMATIC FOLIAGE

Artemisia abrotanum Southernwood
Artemisia absinthium Wormwood
Artemisia arborescens

Caryopteris clandonensis
Choisya ternata Mexican orange blossom
Cistus spp. Rock rose
Elsholtzia stauntonii Mint shrub
Eucalyptus gunnii Cider gum
Laurus nobilis Sweet bay
Lavandula spp. Lavender
Myrica pensylvanica
Myrtus communis Myrtle
Phlomis fruticosa Jerusalem sage
Rosa eglanteria Eglantine
Rosa gallica
Rosmarinus officinalis Rosemary
Ruta graveolens 'Jackman's Blue' Rue
Salvia officinalis Sage
Santolina spp. Cotton lavender
Thymus × *citriodorus* Lemon-scented thyme

UNUSUAL PLANTS FOR CONTAINERS

FERNS

Adiantum pedatum American fern
Athyrium filix-femina Lady fern
Athyrium nipponicum 'Pictum' Japanese painted fern
Dryopteris spp. Shield fern
Matteuccia struthiopteris Ostrich fern
Osmunda regalis Royal fern
Phyllitis scolopendrium (Hart's tongue fern)
Polypodium vulgare Common polypody
Polystichum acrostichoides Christmas fern
Polystichum setiferum Soft shield fern

BAMBOOS AND GRASSES

Agropyron spp. Dog grass
Arundinaria viridistriata Bamboo
Carex morrowii Japanese sedge

Iris hybrid

Phyllitis scolopendrium
(Hart's tongue fern)

Cortaderia selloana Pampas
Deschampsia caespitosa Tufted
 hair grass
Festuca ovina Sheep fescue
Imperata cylindrica 'Rubra'
 Blood grass
Miscanthus sacchariflorus
 Amur silver grass
Molina caerulea 'Variegata'
 Moorgrass
Pennisetum alopecuroides
Spartina pectinata Cordgrass
Stipa gigantea Needlegrass

PLANTS FOR TOPIARY

EVERGREEN PLANTS FOR CLIPPING TO SHAPE

Buxus sempervirens Box
Ilex aquifolium Holly
Ilex crenata Japanese
 holly
Laurus nobilis Sweetbay
Ligustrum ovalifolium Privet
Juniperus spp. Juniper
Myrtus communis Myrtle
Rosmarinus officinalis
 Rosemary
Santolina spp. Cotton lavender
Taxus baccata English yew

PLANTS TO GROW UP PREFORMED WIRE SHAPES

Chrysanthemum × *morifolium*
 Florist's chrysanthemum
Ficus pumila Creeping fig
Hedera helix (small-leaved
 forms) Ivy
Myrtus communis Myrtle

Sempervivum spp. Houseleek
Thymus pseudolanuginosus
 Thyme

PLANTS OF LOOSE GROWTH FOR PRUNING TO SHAPE

Chrysanthemum spp.
Fuchsia hybrids
Hibiscus spp.
Hydrangea paniculata
Lonicera spp. (shrubby forms)
 Honeysuckle

WATER PLANTS

FLOATING AQUATICS (Planting depth 500mm (1 ft 3 in)

Aponogeton distachyus Cape
 pondweed
Azolla caroliniana Mosquito
 plant
Eichhornia crassipes Floating
 water hyacinth
Hydrocharis morsus-ranae
 Frog-bit
Nymphaea hybrids Water lily
Nymphaea candidissima
 (white)
Nymphaea ellisiana (red)
Nymphaea 'Froebelii' (wine-
 red and scented)
Nymphaea 'Graziella'
 (yellow/copper)
Nymphaea odorata 'Rose Arey'
 (pink and scented)
Nymphaea 'William Falconer'
 (ruby-red)
Nymphoides peltata Water-
 fringe
Orontium aquaticum Golden
 club
Stratiotes aloides Water-soldier
Trapa natans Water chestnut
Utricularia vulgaris
 Bladderwort

SUBMERGED OXYGENATORS

Ceratophyllum demersum
 Hornwort
Elodea canadensis Waterweed

Hottonia palustris Water violet
Lagarosiphon muscoides
Myriophyllum spp. Water
 milfoil
Potamogeton crispus Curled
 pondweed
Ranunculus aquatilis Water
 crowfoot

SHALLOW-WATER PLANTS

Acorus calamus Sweet flag
Butomus umbellatus Flowering
 rush
Calla palustris Bog arum
Caltha palustris Marsh
 marigold
Eriophorum spp. Cotton grass
Glyceria spp. Manna grass
Iris laevigata 'Alba'
Iris laevigata 'Variegata'
Iris pseudacorus Yellow flag
Myosotis scorpioides Water
 forget-me-not
Pontederia cordata Pickerel-
 weed
Sagittaria spp. Arrowhead
Scirpus spp. Bulrush
Typha minima Cat-tail

MOISTURE-LOVING WATERSIDE PLANTS

Astilbe × *arendsii*
Hemerocallis spp. Day lily
Hosta spp. Plantain lily
Iris kaempferi Japanese iris
Iris sibirica Siberian iris
Lysichiton americanum Skunk
 cabbage, great bog arum
Peltiphyllum peltatum
 Umbrella plant
Primula florindae Bog primula
Primula japonica Japanese
 primrose

MOISTURE-LOVING FERNS

Blechnum spicant Deer fern
Dryopteris filix-mas Male fern
Matteuccia struthiopteris
 Ostrich fern
Onoclea sensibilis Sensitive
 fern
Osmunda regalis Royal fern
Phyllitis scolopendrium Hart's
 tongue fern

ACKNOWLEDGMENTS

Author's acknowledgments

My erratic life schedule must drive my editors at Dorling Kindersley quite mad. But they unfailingly provide both argument and assent in measured doses and at the appropriate times so that I have the great pleasure of working within a team during production. I would especially like to thank both David Lamb and Rosie Ford to this end, with Alex Arthur the art editor.

At home base my appalling script is patiently and ably interpreted by Caroline Dougan. I thank her also.

Dorling Kindersley would like to thank the following for their help in producing this book: Fiona Macmillan, Sean Moore, Fiona James, Josephine Buchanan, Richard Bird, Kate Grant and Arthur Brown.

Mr and Mrs M. Harty, Mr and Mrs R. Tomosci, Mrs S. M. Evershed, Roger Bristow and Maggie Huscroft, Mr and Mrs P. Holland, Mrs J. A. Holland, Mr and Mrs P. King and Mr and Mrs A. Hobart for letting us photograph their gardens. Hounslow Garden Centre and Jewsons.

Geoff Dann for special photography.

Illustrations by Eric Thomas. Additional illustrations by Sandra Pond, Janos Marffy and Imperial Artists Limited.

Photographic credits

Michael Boys Syndication: 9TR, 12BL, 13, 22L, 25, 30BL, 33, 69, 80BL, 137TL, 140B, 143T, 143BL, 172T, 187.
John Brookes: 42B, 63BR, 66BL, 66BR, 67BR, 73BR, 84TR, 90BR, 95TR, 95TL, 95BM, 105TR, 119TL, 122BL, 131TR, 133TL, 133TR, 134B, 135TL, 146B, 182BR, 186B.
Karl-Dietrich Bühler: 7, 21, 36BR, 61, 70BL, 89, 90BL, 91, 98BR, 114B, 126BL.
Linda Burgess: 24BR, 68BL, 68TR, 82T, 101T.
Karen Bussolini: 76TR.
Camera Press: 8/9T, 10BL, 23, 31B, 32B, 36BL, 104T, 110TR, 110B, 118BR, 129, 130B (photo: Kurt Hansson), 133BL, 136/137B, 142TR.
Eric Crichton Photos: 12BR, 166BL.
Geoff Dann: 2/3, 14B, 15, 16TR, 16BR, 17, 18/19, 20, 38B, 39, 41BR, 43, 46B, 47, 50B, 51, 53BR, 54B, 55, 57BR, 58T, 62T, 64/65, 96, 102/103, 112/113, 116/117, 120/121, 121TL, 147, 149, 150/151, 156B, 162/163, 170/171, 188/189, 190BR.

Everard Reed Gallery (Johannesburg): 135TR.
Neil Holmes Photography: 125BR, 152BR.
Timothy Hursley: 6BL.
Jacqui Hurst: 27T, 96TR, 134TR, 164BL.
Keith Kirften: 131B.
Ken Kirkwood: 107T, 139T, 139BL.
David Lamb: 118TL.
National Trust: 95BR.
John Neubauer: 59, 60B, 78T, 100T, 101B, 105BL, 126BR, 127, 141.
Robert Perron: 80TR, 88B.
Jessica Strang: 8BL, 24BL, 30BR, 74T, 132BR, 133TM.
Oehme Van Sweden & Associates: 124BR.
Pamela Toler (Impact Photos): 9BR, 84BL, 94, 108BL, 109, 115TL, 125T, 133BM.
Volkman K. Wentzel: 115BL.
Elizabeth Whiting Associates: 27B, 73T, 105TL, 122BR, 123B, 128TR, 145, 160BR.
Steve Woodes: 176T.
Josephine Zeitlin: 72BL, 95BL, 108BR (garden design by Michael Bates), 111T, 117T, 138T, 143BR, 178T.